From Venice

to

Venice

Poets of California and Italy

Edited by Mark Lipman and Anna Lombardo

EL MARTILLO PRESS

EL MARTILLO PRESS

From Venice to Venice: Poets of California and Italy
Poems are the property of their prospective authors.
Edited by Mark Lipman and Anna Lombardo.

ISBN: 979-8-8692-4471-0

Published by El Martillo Press
in the United States of America.
elmartillopress.com

Cover by Alessandra Drigo.

Set in Garamond.
Typeset for El Martillo Press by David A. Romero.
davidaromero.com

NOTICE: SCHOOLS AND BUSINESSES
El Martillo Press offers copies of this book at quantity discount with bulk purchase for educational, business, or sales promotional use. For information, please email the publisher at elmartillopress@gmail.com.

VENICE, CA

VENICE, IT

Zingonia Zingone

*All Italian translations are credited to Anna Lombardo, unless noted otherwise

INTRODUCTION
ANNA LOMBARDO

It could only be called *From Venice to Venice*, the poetic collection born from the idea developed in Venice (Italy) with my friend, the poet Matt Sedillo, during the XVII edition of the International Poetry Festival, 'Palabra en el Mundo,' held in Venice in May 2023. This anthological collection has as its generative project that of exchange, knowledge, and mutual gift through the poetic word because we are convinced of poetry's proactive force. It wants to transcend divisions, languages, geographical areas, generational experiences, and poetics. Building a bridge, therefore, despite the geographical distance. A dialogue, a listening to everything around us. From this intersection of sounds, alphabets, and visions of worlds and humanity, the poetic word takes its vital energy. In a world currently on the brink of a nervous crisis that risks falling into a state of no return, for all humanity, this anthological journey is a shining stone, a beacon of hope where poetry vibrates in unison with what it sees, touches, and listens to, since it is not indifferent to the evils and disasters of these derailed times.

The verses of the poets chosen here, with their own poetic individuality, also set in motion the importance of collective action, recalling, in an original way, the preciousness of cross-pollination, of mutual knowledge. In fact, from almost all the poems, the richness of the different existential conditions that cross our lives, emerges. Realities are sometimes painful, bitter, and crude, to which the distorted logic of single thought and the prevailing globalized economy want us to get accustomed to, but which their poetic word bathes and redeems. Finally, this 'anthological' poetic bridge does not forget the beauty surrounding us and quietly reminds us that we are not alone in walking this earth.

Anna Lombardo—Venice (Italy), 12th February 2024

INTRODUZIONE
ANNA LOMBARDO

Non poteva che chiamarsi *From Venice to Venice*, questa raccolta poetica che nasce dall'idea maturata proprio nell'italiana Venezia con l'amico poeta Matt Sedillo durante la XVII edizione del Festival Internazionale di Poesia, Palabra en el Mundo, svoltosi a Venezia nel maggio 2023. Questa raccolta antologica ha come suo progetto generativo quello dello scambio, della conoscenza, del dono reciproco attraverso la parola poetica perché siamo convinti della forza propositiva che la poesia ha. Essa vuole trascendere divisioni, lingue, aree geografiche, esperienze generazionali diverse, nonché poetiche differenti. Gettare un ponte, quindi, nonostante la distanza geografica. Un dialogo, un ascolto verso tutto ciò che attorno ci circonda. Da questo incrocio di suoni, alfabeti e visioni di mondi ed umanità la parola poetica prende la sua energia vitale. In un mondo attualmente sull'orlo di una crisi nervosa che rischia di precipitare in un non ritorno, per l'umanità intera, questo percorso antologico è una pietra lucente, un faro di speranza dove la poesia vibra all'unisono con ciò che vede, tocca e ascolta, poiché essa non è indifferente ai mali e ai disastri di questi tempi deragliati.

I versi dei poeti qui scelti, con la propria individualità poetica, rimettono in moto anche l'importanza del fare collettivo, richiamando, in modo originale, la preziosità della contaminazione, della conoscenza reciproca. Da quasi tutte le poesie, infatti, mi pare proprio emerga la ricchezza delle diverse condizioni esistenziali che attraversano le nostre vite.

Realtà, a volte sofferte, amare, crude a cui le logiche distorte del pensiero unico e della economia globalizzata imperante ci vogliono abituare ma che la loro parola poetica, nella loro tessitura articolata, irrora e riscatta. Questo ponte poetico 'antologico', infine, non dimentica il bello che ci circonda e ci ricorda sommessamente che non siamo da soli a camminare su questa terra.

Anna Lombardo—Venezia (Italia), 12 Febbraio 2024

INTRODUCTION
MARK LIPMAN

Venice, CA: A Place Unlike Any Other

Firstly, I'd like to thank Richard Modiano for his invaluable assistance in gathering these poems [for the Venice, CA section] to bring together some of the most prominent voices in our Venice community, as well as from Beyond Baroque, which has been home to the literary arts and so much more in Venice, since its founding by George Drury Smith in1968.

There are certain places in this world that call to you, that you feel an immediate connection to, that whether you've been born and raised there, or only been around for a minute, you know that you belong. That was the immediate vibe I felt on the day I arrived in Venice, California.

It's something that you cannot buy, or put a price tag on, and those who try, no matter how big their mansions, no matter how tall they try to build their walls, no matter how much they try to make it all fit, moving in like settlers with selfie sticks, you can't buy cool, or be part of a community by trying to erase it.

You see, Venice, CA, the real Venice, CA, has a reputation. "Venice is where art meets crime." That's the way it is and it's not about being criminal, but about not being afraid to get your hands dirty and roll through the back alleys of life, and to push back when it becomes necessary… Because Venice is about being real, it's about community, and that's where art thrives.

The voice of the artist, the poet, must have that edge to it, and in Venice it's a literal beachhead, a vanguard for creativity and critical thinking, with a generational history unique to itself that has carried the torch of poetry with it since the early days of its founding, envisioned by Abbott Kinney as a canal-laced homage to its namesake in Italy.

To list here all the great talent Venice has been home to and inspired over the years, would simply be too many to mention. What we can do though is add another page, another chapter, to the continuing story, to keep that torch lit until the poets of tomorrow are ready to lift it.

In this selection we find some of the most notable torchbearers of poetry our Venice community has to offer and it's my honor to present them to you here.

VENICE, CA

Writer, artist, philosopher, and pianist **Will Alexander** was born in Los Angeles, California in 1948 and has remained a lifetime resident of the city. He earned a BA in English and creative writing from the University of California–Los Angeles in 1972. Alexander's over two dozen books of poetry include Across the Vapour Gulf (2017), Compression & Purity (2011), The Sri Lankan Loxodrome (2009), Asia & Haiti (1995), and The Stratospheric Canticles (1995). He has taught at many colleges and universities, including the Jack Kerouac School of Disembodied Poetics, the University of California, and Hofstra University, among others. His collection *Singing In Magnetic Hoofbeat: Essays, Prose, Texts, Interviews, and a Lecture* (2013) was awarded an American Book Award. Alexander was a 2022 finalist for the Pulitzer Prize. His other honors include a Whiting Fellowship for Poetry, a California Arts Council Fellowship, and the 2016 Jackson Poetry Prize.

Re-expanded Hamlet

Blaze being maniacal saffron
not simply due to mirage as transport
as debility masquerading as simplistic hamlet
being seismic saffron as transport
that summons disabled beckoning
via mottled strategic import
as designated grammar
as proto-physicality
as hieroglyphic
as margin
being designated nostrum helical in nature
so that light is emitted by blazes
so that curious transport transpires
being postulate by hurricane
by aerial sub-atomic
being living phoneme via symbol
so that symbol remains endemic
not as postulate
but by aerial sub-atomic
being riotous symbol that mesmerises
by taxonomy that persists
that transmutes by its own kinetic
by wizardry that transports
by calm as emetic power

The Inhuman As Velocity

for Andrew Joron

Blue eroded suns that eclipse
their own innateness as madrigal
at velocities that seem to repeal evolutionary essence
not simply concerning there own eruption but as occulted
      force fields
that renew their own occulted essence

Subtended Mazes

Perhaps pending splendiferous maze
being principle atom as novae
being lenticular crown
being atomic preconsistency as domain
as ashen cannibals' property
that ironically reflects ashen solar form as capacity
that reflects dour ancestral hours
being maze of itself
that remains presence as complication
that reinstates its own mesmerics
as primordial flare
as primeval reflectivity
being darkened particle that reflects its own gaze
as drift
as culminate hesitation
that explodes its own drift
its own culminate hesitation
not as embrangled circumference
as positionless zeal
but as rhetoric that scatters
& subtends mazes

Voltage By Perspicacity

This being incident as perpendicular property
as higher owl that stratifies itself
as higher incident
as mural
as happenstance this being nausea
that Breton proclaimed as Nadja
as surreptitious
as boiling electrical amount
that fails to gather its own fatigue
as it smoulders & erupts its own blizzard
its gathered amount
as pronouncement that splinters
& avails itself
as illuminated transmission
as fresh & splendoured dazzling
not as conscripted flask
or hierarchal invasion
but mask as moss
as fabulous babbling
prone to its own beclouded merit

never as monoculture by plague or triangulation exposure
not inversion that ignites its own milestones according to task
          it blackened its own millstone
& blackens its own dust
& proclaims its own strategic animation
as phantom
as charitable coffin being dove
as arch-ridiculous phantasm

being kinetic by transparence
by transparent fatigue
as fire tonic
as glistening novae by ash

perhaps a glimmering novae as riddle
that resists its own confusion
that surmounts itself via former implosion being higher task
being voltage by perspicacity

Spell As Pluperfect Unitary Radiance

Being none other than Unitary oracle
as transfixed splaying
as hidden misnomer
that fractiously displays its own grandeur
as if it were scale as protracted nimbus
as lightning glyph
as oracle
not as maimed significance
perhaps a solar field that registers
perhaps phoneme as lowered density
possibly a graph that inertly blazes
that calms its own fractionation
being the human state as boundless character
being a relay of suns
not an array of glimmers as phonemic pyroclastics
but as peril that anointed its own power
as array
as signal by possibility
as significance by mutable character
self-igniting its own array
not challenge by human optimum
but explosive human circuit that ignites
as perfect characterological reference
not as grandiose moral or transfixed complacency
but as resplendent poise as balanced containment
this being bodiless arcana
as cosmically renowned confiding in itself existing
as an array of seedings
having transfixed their own coloration

not as unclaimed pattern or debility by
or integer
or by path that clears its own corruption by circuitous moral
by extended fragment
as dust by fractious power
as summoned bewailing
according to summoned primeval
sans geriatric moral
as bodiless moral
not as by integer
according to mysterious force or heralded primeval
there exists no geriatric proclamation
as wizened plane
or structured co-evidence
that graphs its own summoning
that anointed its own pre-figurement
not by hamlet
or combustion
or fatigue
not as disabled neural alignment
or simulation by photographic drill
or seismic pre-aperture
as dust during nightfall
or precipitous moon rain
neither this or that phantom
baffling the Milky Way

Iris Berry is the co-founder of Punk Hostage Press. She is the author and editor of several books and has a vast fan base for her unique voice and formidable writing style. She's an L.A. Pop culture historian, actress, and musician. She's appeared in numerous films, TV commercials, documentaries, and iconic rock videos. In the 1980s & 90s, she sang, performed, wrote songs and recorded with the Lame Flames, the Ringling Sisters, the Dickies, the Flesh Eaters, and Pink Sabbath. She served four years on the Board of Directors for Beyond Baroque Literary/Arts Center. In 2009 she received her 2nd Certificate of Merit Award from the city of Los Angeles for her contribution as a Los Angeles writer, and for her extensive charity work. Iris continues to champion and advocate for original voices. Books by Iris Berry: *All That Shines Under The Hollywood Sign, The Daughters of Bastards, The Trouble with Palm Trees* and *Gas Station Etiquette.*

PORTRAIT OF MY LOS ANGELES...

It's the earthquake weather in me
It's my love for palm trees
and the way they line certain streets.

My love for supermarkets
with their big empty parking lots

It's taking long drives
through various canyons

It's being in love with
certain silhouettes and views
of trees and telephone poles
as the sun sets behind them
because I've seen them
all my life
and they're embedded in my soul.

It's having love for certain streets
because they have no sidewalks.

It's my ability to love the ocean
only through a restaurant window
but disliking it with its direct Sun
if asked to lay in it
scantily clad
for more than 2 minutes.

It's my love for the stars

the ones in the sky
and on sidewalks.

It's growing up with an empty backyard
and having to drive far
to visit friends and family.

It's only knowing the changing seasons
by what's on display
on the shelves at the supermarkets.

It's having to drive everywhere
just to get anywhere.
It's being bummed when it rains
even though there's a drought.

It's talking on the phone with friends
more than seeing them in person.

It's my love for the beach
but rarely seeing it.

It's being guilty of saying,
"it's hot but it's a dry heat."

It's refusing to go somewhere because,
I probably won't find a place to park,
and yet there are parking lots everywhere.

It's all the famous streets and boulevards
with their incredible history.

It's the many different cultures
and subcultures and cults.

It's the place where people
come to *Be Somebody.*

It's definitely a love/hate thing.
Sometimes it's like the greatest drug
and the best place on earth
and sometimes it's like telling someone
you love them and they don't say it back.

But it's my home
I was born here
I can't imagine living anywhere else
I can't imagine
leaving Los Angeles…

AS GOOD AS IT GETS

In the past few years
I've learned
that just because you're
loyal
honest
and devoted
does not mean
it will be reciprocated.
That sometimes
sadly
no good deed
goes unpunished.
And most movies
do not resemble
real life
especially the ones
with the big budgets.
And what my grandmothers
told me about men
is true.

I've also learned
that no matter how much
you know and love somebody
they can still have secrets
that could break your heart
and possibly kill you.

I've also learned
don't rely on fortune cookies
but never let
a good wishbone
go to waste.

That nothing is personal
and everything is personal
no one is perfect
especially me
and the more mistakes
I make
the more human and nice
I am towards you
and the more powerful
I think
I am
the more danger
I am in.

I've learned
that everyone dies
some quickly
some slowly
so it's best
to live
the life
you really want
It's taken me forever
to realize
that I still haven't
grown-up

and that
somehow
I still have the fantasy
that as long
as I am
a good person
life will get better.

But what I've really learned is
the clock is tick tick ticking
and maybe
I should
do my best
to leave this place
with a smile on my face
and love in my heart
for you
and for me
and maybe that's
as good
as it gets
and if that's the case
I will
consider myself
lucky…

S.A. Griffin lives, loves, and works in Los Angeles. Publishing on his own Rose of Sharon imprint since 1988, he is the editor of *The Official Language of Yes!* (Perceval Press) by Scott Wannberg, co-editor of *The Outlaw Bible of American Poetry* (Thunder's Mouth Press) for which he received the Firecracker Award and *Beat Not Beat* (Moon Tide Press). Published widely, he is most recently the author of *Pandemic Soul Music* (Punk Hostage Press). Carma Bum, father, husband, cat lover and Vietnam era veteran of the USAF.

Confessions of a Door to Door Autographed Outlaw Bible Salesman

guns, knives, speed, weed, bald ass lies,
fast cars, dice, junk, mad sex, porn and drunken orgies
will never make anyone an honest outlaw
however, any or all might bring on a sad liver,
a failed kidney, an exploding ticker, rusty veins, no credit,
a flipped wig, a bitter ex and/or a
same sex love affair with the law

most of what is sacred in our
bastard world of
poetry and small press
is not and never was

cool

a cultural malignancy
and artistic anomaly of
puking conformity

there are giddy exceptions tho
generally predicated upon single expression
or vision and nothing else

what makes cool is the
same thing that
might make hip

it just is

like d.a. levy of Cleveland
simply who and what they are
outside the margins
maverick
by necessity

whose only victory might be to declare
what would be their genius

all those that follow with their nostrils flaring up their
false gods' fetid asses in search of lost cities
are foolish fashion mongers pressing themselves into
unforgiving clichés

I cannot remember where
HST or Bukowski ever
wrote or said, *this is the way*

mostly what they said if anything
was straight ahead, *this is my way*
like Anais inside the
top down of her soft parade

the mystery and magic of the grape
will not make you a writer
posing in black ether with your hands
jammed into your pockets
leaning against bearded time
will not make you a poet

like most everyone else

in this changing city I am a sincere liar
guilty of some small
crimes of fashion

this is one of them

a low rider on the apocalypse
haunted by long haired dreams of being
born again as a rock star

honestly, I don't know what
makes a poet, but they
are among us

a little outlaw dancing
in every one

Mein Trump

these words might be viewed as a broken mirror
a possible reflection of our changing world
a shifting allegory of mixed feelings
wedded to select history
tightly woven into
discordant
partisan
      warps

a flux of fevered minds
before the nervous pyramids
of a rising tyranny

a stitch in time
      caught
between text
      commentary
and a
      clear eye

an intoxicating echo chamber of communal blackmail
made mad by the electric spectacle of a republic
split into feudal factions

a televised diary of pain collapsing beneath
a staggering reality show of processed imagination
alternative facts and
misplaced loyalties

set in stone

the revolutionary engines of now
roaring a counterfeit oratory of blind faith
to the cheap seats

the drowning soul of our frenzied nature
mired in a quarrelsome hope beyond reason
our calls for justice falling on the
deaf ears of an apathetic Congress
locked in a legislative minstrel show of
choreographed failure to orphan our daily bread

the waving wheat of future generations
clashing in a perennial fiction to secure
sacred borders inked in blood
and bound by murder

America, you dead hippie
older, but no wiser
there's red lipstick on your collar

you have become a blue movie of yourself
an embarrassing pornography of riches
a sexist horse opera of reckless enthusiasm
a capitalist slumlord caught in the malignant spin
of an old realm splendor

your ancient bigotries dancing a nervous breakdown
of whitewashed nostalgia
tired tales told and retold as race baiting atomic reminders

of spiritual union and glorious rebirth

a digital wildfire hardwired behind the rapid eyes
of a sleeping nation dreaming from a cup half full
of a past poorly remembered
promising a return to some
old Kentucky home
that never was

the working poor frozen in the pitch of their nightmare reality
lost between entertaining themselves to death
and the deep focus of a fat city on a hill strutting a
perpendicular demonstration of dysfunctional brilliance
pimping a rapid-fire charm of privilege from the twilight mud
where your wretched refuse seek shelter
caught in the vice of a superficial sentimentality
married to passion on the verge of tears
deep sixing any chance of a life lived without care
        the ordinary genius of what living ought to be

our great cities a paved tangle of sprawling gentrification
shedding their skins in a strike of hypnotizing light
a witch hunting beacon of certain security
that cripples all pity with the graciously patronizing attitudes
of a vertically integrated state held spellbound
by a sanctioned hyperbole of day for night

talking heads in a decapitated theatre of
missed cues and deaf dialogue
that repeats itself indifferently

the bleeding edge of scripted hatred and outrage

immigrant song flees native destiny
severed by paralyzing conceptions of class
reborn forever speechless as intuition reconciled in despair
the origins of the deplorable deplorables

the tired and poor taken in by a winking treasury of
security at the apple's eye only to destroy them
with their core desire to live in plenty

exiles reaching for a future balanced before them
like a postcard from the edge
in the hardly enough light

all eyes open to the fading memory
of life as a worker
a willfully neglected once and future fable
burning with impatience
for those who wish to
beat feet to a better life

refugee America, call home your rebel patriots
celebrate your revolutionary progeny marked
by their contagious activism and unshakable determination
to recast the narrative as a magnificent bright nova
of loving relief under an honest sun
to cure every malevolent branch of night

our wise minorities knighted by a renewed resolve
to abolish the degradation of the individual
the liberated better angels of the self
no longer shackled by guilt

soar with the ideal tenacity of a child to destroy
those social tumors rooted in dystopian fairy tales
of self-preservation

death peace takes the dispossessed into her
begging embrace at the gates of sorrow

caged children cut down to ragged shoots and weeds
at the border of hope

shadows cast against the memories of meadows
rest uneasy inside the heart of darkness
where the war is never over

mongrel America, author of
every lost cause you'll
never find

who are we now all grown up
sitting before the starry candles
burning on our cake

thoughts and prayers
with the gravest of consequences
as we ignore the symptoms
only to become
the disease

Susan Hayden is a multigenre writer, published in the anthologies *Beat Not Beat* (Moon Tide Press); *Los Angeles In the 1970s: Weird Scenes Inside the Goldmine* (Rare Bird Books); *The Black Body* (Seven Stories Press), *I Might Be The Person You Are Talking To* (Padua Playwrights Press) and elsewhere. She is the creator, curator and producer of Library Girl, a words + music literary series. Originating in 2009 at the Ruskin Group Theatre in Santa Monica, CA, the show celebrates the written word and features poets, essayists, novelists, playwrights, and singer-songwriters. In 2015, she received the Bruria Finkel/Artist in the Community Volunteerism Award from the Santa Monica Arts Foundation, for her significant contributions to the energetic discourse within Santa Monica's arts community. Hayden is also a playwright. Her work has been produced at The MET Theatre, Padua Playwrights Festival, Mark Taper Forum's Other Voices, Lost Studio, South Coast Repertory's Nexus Project, Ensemble Studio Theatre's WinterFest, The California Studies Council, and Café Plays at the Ruskin. Hayden is the proud mother of singer-songwriter Mason Summit, who performs with Irene Greene in the angsty Americana duo, The Prickly Pair. She lives in Santa Monica with her husband, music journalist Steve Hochman. *Now You Are a Missing Person* is her first published book.

The Game of Belief

(1989)

I used to be a believer,
believed in the voodoo of mortal witches,
the power of myth and incantation
in everyday existences,
total honesty
at the cost of losing
a potential friend or lover
and in monogamy
at the cost of losing you.
I believed in the geometry of surrender,
the cadence of ash
and in the commonality
of domestic vaudeville acts.
I believed in the geography
of sacrifice and bliss,
the histrionics of self-deception
and fighting for inner peace
until I became an activist
in my own war of remembrance
and lost.
I believed in the low cost of simple tasks
performed daily
though they negated the cause and effect,
the natural process—
the faith of blind men
who could still see me
and the clarity of those
who couldn't.

Maybe all that I've given up over the years
is a game I must re-learn.

But What About Odetta?

our son asked,
when I told him
his father was missing
in the snow.
She was his favorite singer,
this was to be her final tour.
She was seventy-seven.
He was eleven.
We had tickets to see her
in concert that night,
had been planning it
for months.
He cried when I told him
we couldn't go.

Our son was used to
his father taking off
to the woods
or the rocks,
some river or slope.
He could be late,
get lost sometimes
or snowed in
but he'd always find us
and catch up to whatever
we had planned.

Our son asked if his father
could just meet us

at McCabe's
when he got home.
But I had to say "No,
this is more serious."
I needed to drive
to Mountain High
while listening to
car-radio news updates.
I needed to wait there
for my husband,
for his father
to be found,
one way or the other.

Our son asked,
when I got home,
if he could sleep
in the bed with me.
He knew they'd called off
the search
and his father was
still missing.
"When will he be back?"
he asked repeatedly.
I lit a candle,
turned out the lights.
From the bed,
when I looked up at
the ceiling,
I could have sworn
I'd seen the shadow
of a skier,

climbing uphill.

Our son was half-asleep
when I said,
"I don't have
a good feeling
about this."
I held him in my arms
for hours. Only
these days,
when he tells the story,
he doesn't even remember
my being there.
In the middle of the night,
I knelt in the kitchen
singing an Odetta song,
"Hit or Miss,"
trying to find comfort in
her rejoicing.
And finally, I stood over
the trash can,
tore up
the concert tickets.

Ellyn Maybe has performed her poetry all over the country, including Bumbershoot, the Poetry Project, the New School, Taos Poetry Circus, South by Southwest, Lollapalooza, Albuquerque Poetry Festival and Seattle Poetry Festival. She has also read in Europe at the Bristol Poetry Festival, on the BBC, and in poetry slams and readings in Munich, Frankfurt, Hamburg and Stuttgart. She opened the MTV Spoken Wurd Tour in Los Angeles. In addition, she has also read at USC, UCLA, CSUN, and Cal State Fullerton, among other colleges. *Writer's Digest* named her one of ten poets to watch in the new millennium. Her work has been included in many anthologies, including *Word Warriors: 35 Women Leaders in the Spoken Word Revolution, Poetry Slam, Another City: Writing From Los Angeles, Poetry Nation, The Outlaw Bible of American Poetry and American Poetry: The Next Generation.* She was on the 1998 and 1999 Venice Beach Slam teams. She was seen reading her work in Michael Radford's (*Il Postino*) film *Dancing at the Blue Iguana.*

Someday Our Peace Will Come

one day poetry dropped from the sky
and the animals grew iambic pentameter tails
and the people breathed in stars

one day music dropped from the sky
and the architecture turned symphonic
and the people breathed in harmony

one day memory dropped from the sky
and the past present and future sifted like flour
and the people breathed in wonder

smoke and ash
as distant as two sides of the same coin

Eternal Eponine

If you've seen Les Mis you know what I mean.
If you've been to high school you also know.
Life is a musical on the very best days.
Life is a musical on the very worse days.
Musicals walk our emotions on the slippery emotional slope of
      childhood.
Weirdness, Defiance, Acceptance, and the Wisdom to know
      you are the difference.
Life is a theatrical terrain and we break the 4th wall carrying a
      curtain and a ghost light.
Breakfast is full on pancake makeup.
Lunch is props from The Apple Orchard.
My Dinner is with Andre.
I'm Eternal Eponine,
The most reliable narrator I've ever seen.

While a resident of New York City **Richard Modiano** became active in the literary community connected to the Poetry Project where he came to know Gregory Corso, Allen Ginsberg, Anne Waldman, William S. Burroughs, and Ted Berrigan. Modiano served on the board of directors of Valley Contemporary Poets from 1995 until 2001. In 2001 he was a programmer at Beyond Baroque Literary/Arts Center, joined the Board of Trustees in 2006, and from 2010 to 2019, he served as Executive Director. In that time, he produced and curated hundreds of literary events, and with Henry Morro, Suzanne Lummis, and Liz Camfiord co-founded and named Beyond Baroque Books' sub-imprint The Pacific Coast Poetry Series. In 2019 he was elected Vice President of the California State Poetry Society. In 2023 Modiano joined the board of directors of the Los Angles Poetry Society. *The Huffington Post* named him as one of 200 people doing the most to promote poetry in the United States. In 2022 the Los Angeles-Long Beach Harbor Labor Coalition awarded Modiano the Joe Hill Prize for labor poetry and was a Pushcart Prize nominee. His collection *The Forbidden Lunch Box* is published by Punk Hostage Press. Richard is a rank and file member of the Industrial Workers of the World and a member of the National Writers Union.

When He Comes for Me

Rimbaud knew better than
to save any of himself for the grave—
He spent every resource to the last penny—
He burned
money, health, friends, family, sanity
as so much fuel for the fire—

When Death came to take the poet
He got nothing, not even a man
with his pride or common sense intact—

When He comes for me
What will He find?

Poet, editor, publisher, scholar, and critic, **Bill Mohr** is widely recognized as one of the leading literary activists in Southern California in the past 40 years. His writing has been featured in over a dozen anthologies, and translated into Spanish, Japanese, Italian, and Croatian. His work as editor/publisher of Momentum Press received four awards from the National Endowment for the Arts, and his honors include being a visiting scholar at the Getty Research Institute in Los Angeles and fellowships at the Huntington Library. His highly praised account of West Coast poetry, *Holdouts: The Los Angeles Poetry Renaissance 1948-1992*, was published by the University of Iowa Press in 2011. He is a professor in the Department of English at California State University, Long Beach.

WHY THE HEART NEVER DEVELOPS CANCER

One of the mysteries of the body is why the heart does not develop cancer. Every other organ in the body—stomach, skin, brain, lungs, liver—can develop cancer, but the heart squeezes itself again and again without the least trace of malignancy. It is as though the heart is a furnace and anything cancerous which enters is immediately consumed by the heat of its pulse. On the other hand, the only pleasure the heart receives is imaginary. The skin, the stomach, the lungs—all these organs are capable of enjoying sensual life: the warmth of the sun, a feast of vegetables and turkey, a good smoke, and therefore they are more vulnerable. The heart has only our blood to be its companion. Blood, like the heart, receives no direct pleasure and it brings no relief to the heart, which denies that the body it inhabits means anything more than a warm place to work. The heart, like the life-force itself, is absolutely impersonal. The heart does not care what happens to the body. It is there to work as hard as possible for as long as possible and in return for the body's acceptance of its indifferent loyalty, it never betrays the body by consuming itself cell by cell

TOMATO SKINS

My mother called and said a tiny flap
of tomato skin was stuck inside her throat
the way a child who crawled too far might be
irreversibly encased in a mining shaft.
Portable generators! All night stand by!
I don't believe she ever again trusted
unpeeled tomatoes. A day or two after,
she called to tell of watching a butterfly
tunnel through her garden, and how a jay
swooped in and netted its flight
in a perishing knot so deft as to yank
invisibility: now that my mother's dead,
and I don't have to call her once a day
to see if she's clamped down on something
unextractable, some taut tarpaulin
of indissoluble paradox, I remember how much
she wanted at the end to fossilize her life again,
with nothing in its misery altered in the least,
not even when she was sobbing at the end of a hall,
"You kids will kill me yet. You kids will kill me yet."
But she can't live it again, nor can my brothers
or sisters; I wonder if any of this infundibular
rejectamenta ever existed. There, the crescent.
There, the swallowing, with no return.

Harry E. Northup has made a living as an actor for 30 years, acting in 37 films and 43 television shows. Harry has been a member of the Academy of Motion Picture Arts and Sciences since 1976. Harry is that rare American actor who is also an accomplished poet. He has had twelve books of poetry published: *Amarillo Born* (Victor Jiminez Press, 1966); *the jon voight poems* (Mt. Alverno Press, 1973); *Eros Ash* (Momentum Press, 1976); *Enough The Great Running Chapel* (Momentum Press, 1982); *the images we possess kill the capturing* (the jesse press, 1988); *The Ragged Vertical* (Cahuenga Press, 1996); *Reunions* (Cahuenga Press, 2001); *Greatest Hits, 1966-2001* (Pudding House Press, 2002); *Red Snow Fence* (Cahuenga Press, 2006), *Where Bodies Again Recline* (Cahuenga Press, 2011,) *East Hollywood: Memorial to Reason* (Cahuenga Press, 2015) and *Love Poem to MPTF* (Cahuenga Press, 2020.) Harry received his B.A. in English from California State University, Northridge, where he studied verse with Ann Stanford.

Make a poem

Make a poem from pavement, fragmented & black, uneven,
    broken.

Make a poem from an experience, memory, grief.
Make an email a poem.
Make a poem from tweets, write it at intervals,
over a day.

Make a poem from death & hunger.
Make a poem out of embracing a fear.
Make a poem out of wanting to tell someone something.
Make a poem out of fear, vulnerability, poverty of spirit.

Make a poem from poems that you've read.
Poems come from poems.
Read the Language school poets as well as the romantic poets.
While you struggle with learning the many forms,
learn the tradition of poetry, especially the epics.

Make a poem from tennis, sweet potatoes & ruin.
Make a poem from beauty & disgrace.
Make a poem from bowing down to a greater craftsman.
Make a poem out of women & men & trees
with jacaranda blossoms fallen on the sidewalk.
Make a poem from hills & viaduct & sod houses &
country roads & a 2 story red brick schoolhouse.
Out of pride & discounted emotions, make a poem at evening.

(5/23/13)

With Saintliness

With sainted water
With faraway canoe
With tremulous care
With sainted oars
With sainted light
With joy saintliness
With focused centre
With sainted arrows
With sainted circle
With sainted closing
With joining light
With saving hand
With sainted blemish
With circumference blue
With climbing saintliness
With joy eliminated
With saintliness diffused
With sainted hope
With closing hand
With sainted mouth
With joining hearts
With shining road
With long gone cascade
With sainted sound
With sainted search
With saintly doom
With connected light
With sainted substance
With light flowing down   (8/17/17)

Night Light

What is a life but a home & a wife?
What is a home but a son & a book?
What is a book but a poem & a picture?
What is a friend but one who helps?
What is a friend but a window & a door?
What door looks within?
What window takes one away from looking within?
What is a wife but a window within?
What is a night but a place to write?
What is a writer but one who looks within?
What is within but a place to be alone?
To be alone with words with little light.
To be in little light & still see words.
Words are a home.
Words create a home.
A home has light within.
A light that does not gossip.
A word within light bestows home.
What is a home without light?
What is light without words?
What words within bring peace?
What is home but light & love?

(8/26/17)

L.A. native, **Pam Ward** recently released her first poetry book, *between good men & no man at all*, World Stage Press. Pam is the author of two novels, *Want Some Get Some* (Kensington), chronicling a heist after the '92 riots and *bad girls burn slow* (Kensington), a tale of a mother working funeral homes. A UCLA graduate and recipient of a "California Arts Council Fellow" and a Pushcart Prize Nominee, Pam edited the first anthology of Los Angeles black women poets entitled, *The Supergirls Handbook*. While operating a design studio and teaching at Art Center College of Design, Pam merged writing and graphics to produce *My Life, LA* documenting Black Angelinos in poster/stories. Pam's literary showcase, *I Didn't Survive Slavery For This!* a multi-media poetic riff on life post emancipation, featured a collective of poets of The World Stage. Pam currently designs, runs her community imprint Short Dress Press and hosts Beyond Baroque's Wednesday Night Poetry Workshop, the longest running workshop in Los Angeles. Pam recently completed her third novel *Bury My Dress on Central Ave.*, about her aunt's connection to the Black Dahlia murder, a crime so horrific it shocked the whole world happening inside Pam's very own hometown.

Exhaust

She detested it.
Right down to the
ride up there.
Counting Denny's
signs and cars
broke down.
The fake Aztec
look of the suburbs.
It reminded her
of thin
see-through
curtains
chipped
rotten tile
that smoky
dead smell
of motel rooms.
And why
she left him
for good
she thought
that time
all the busted
up plates
stacks of
ripped pictures
her good dresses
shoved in

the trash can.
How he called
her again
and again
'til she finally
picked up
his voice
in one smog
oozing plea.
And the only
thing worse
the only thing
worse than
that dry
separation
was being
with him now
on this hot
vinyl seat
on another
long ride to
his mother's.

Single Mom

Somewhere between
a burnt marriage
a greasy kitchen
and a grey 22.
Sandwiched between
these smiling kids
and my painted teeth.
Somewhere way off
from coffee mugs
stained with yesterday's
paycheck, rent due
that last final kiss.
Choosing between
Disneyland or
Sybil Brand*
murder or Mr.
Toad's ride.
Driving all the way
from Anaheim to LA
anxious as an inmate.
Passing your house
your new car
your girlfriend's red bike
smashing the snails
on my porch.
Somewhere between
what I didn't say
and my black
Ajax mouth

scrounging for words
but spitting a shoe.
With two of you
in my back seat
sweet dreamy lugs
tasting of grape juice
and cherry.
Somewhere between
their breath at my neck
or them asking for water
or the fear
they'll call some
bimbo mommie
gnaws at me yanks
me straight back
from the brink
makes me face
one more sink
full of dishes.

*Sybil Brand was the name of a women's prison in Los Angeles.

Gail Wronsky is the author, coauthor, or translator of sixteen books of poetry and prose, including *Under the Capsized Boat We Fly: New & Selected Poems* (White Pine Press, 2021) and the poetry collections *Imperfect Pastorals*; *Poems for Infidels*; and *Dying for Beauty*, a finalist for the Western Arts Federation Poetry Prize. She is the translator of Argentinean poet Alicia Partnoy's book *Fuegos Florales/Flowering Fires*, winner of the American Poetry Prize from Settlement House Press. Her poems have appeared in many journals, including *Poetry, Boston Review, Antioch Review, Denver Quarterly, Poetry International, Guesthouse,* and *Volt.* Gail is the recipient of an Artists Fellowship from the California Arts Council. Her work has appeared in several anthologies, including *Pratik, the LA Issue; Poets Against War; The Black Body; In Possession of Shakespeare; The Poet's Child; Wide Awake: The Poetry of Los Angeles and Beyond,* and *Coiled Serpent: Poets Arising from the Cultural Quakes and Shifts of Los Angeles. The Moose in the Moon,* her book of poetry for children, was published by Tsehai Publishers. Gail is coeditor of the anthology *What Falls Away is Always: Writers Over 60 on Writing & Death* (What Books Press, 2021). She taught creative writing and women's literature at Loyola Marymount University in Los Angeles where she was awarded the Harry M. Daum Professorship.

We were all ravenous as wolves in those days

Those days seemed to shed
sheets of silver metal,
to crackle like tinfoil. And grass was greener then—
greener even
than the amazement we felt about everything.

Now we find ourselves, as in a sad poem, near reservoirs
burning with late-twilight fire,
still searching for that single word our lips form

when breath passes across these pages
and the specter of a melody remembered from some other
life lifts the words up briefly, like now.

The blinding noise of the day

I hate waking up in the morning

with wings—having given birth

to an egg the size of a small VW.

Don't you?

I grope and sniff,

lost already somewhere

in the blinding noise of the day.

I call and no one answers. It's been

a while since even the wind wrapped me

up in obsessive caresses.

Listener, you think that

this poem will end with me

returning to my bedroom, which

glows like the inside of a lemon and is

carpeted in tiny golden feathers. It does.

VENICE, IT

Giovanni Luca Asmundo, (Palermo, 1987) lives in Venice, where he obtained a Doctorate at the University IUAV. He works in architecture, research, and in teaching.

Published poetry collections: *Trittico d'esordio* ["Debut tryptich"] edited by A. M. Curci (Cofine, 2017); *Stanze d'isola* ["The rooms on the island"] (Oèdipus, 2018) with which he won the Felix Prize; *Disattese - coro di donne mediterranee* ["Neglected - choir of Mediterranean women"] (Versante Ripido, 2019) winner of the Versante Ripido prize; and *Lacerti di coro* ["Fragments of Choir"] (Il Convivio, 2022) winner of the Pietro Carrera prize.

Some of his lyrics and fictional prose appear in magazines and literary blogs. He is one of the founders of the project (photos and poetry), "Topography of a loss," on the sinking of Sicily's Graham Island. He also promotes writing and media projects on various issues connected to migration, reflections, and dialogues about the care of places, cities, and contemporary landscapes, as in his project, "Periplus of the Maritime Republics or of the Open Ports." In his blog, *Peripli*, he collects various columns on those specific topics.

Giovanni Luca Asmundo, (Palermo, 1987) vive a Venezia, dove ha conseguito il Dottorato presso l'Università IUAV; si occupa di architettura, ricerca e didattica.
Raccolte di poesie pubblicate: *Trittico d'esordio* a cura di A. M. Curci (Cofine, 2017); *Stanze d'isola* (Oèdipus, 2018), con cui ha vinto il Premio Felix; *Disattese - coro di donne mediterranee* (Versante Ripido, 2019), vincitore del premio Versante Ripido, e *Lacerti di coro* (Il Convivio, 2022), vincitore del premio Pietro Carrera.

Alcuni dei suoi testi e della sua prosa immaginaria compaiono su riviste e blog letterari. È tra i fondatori del progetto (poesia e foto), "Topografia di una perdita" su un'isola in dissolvenza della Sicilia. Promuove inoltre progetti di scrittura e media su diverse tematiche legate alle migrazioni, riflessioni e dialoghi sulla cura dei luoghi, delle città e dei paesaggi contemporanei, come nel suo progetto "Periplo delle Repubbliche Marinare o dei Porti Aperti". Nel suo blog, Peripli, raccoglie varie rubriche su quegli argomenti specifici.

Lampedusa, October 3rd 2013

If it were only a refulgent bronze statue
like that young man dancing
everything that is now caught fishing
in this stretch of blinding sea.

(in *Lacerti di coro*, Il Convivio, 2022)

Lampedusa, 3 ottobre 2013

Se solo fosse statua di fulgido bronzo
come quel giovinetto danzante
tutto quello che viene ripescato
in questo tratto di mare accecante.

(in *Lacerti di coro*, Il Convivio, 2022)

If waiting, we lose our hair

If waiting, we lose our hair
if the undertow knots our legs
full of salt and wrinkled with age
if sinking with our ankles in cold slime
we'll be the root of shortcomings

veiled, we will wait on the shores
for the bitter return of lost things
until the fingers become fishbones.
The sea plants bodies
and germinates stars.

(in *Disattese - coro di donne mediterranee*, Versante Ripido, 2019)

Se aspettando perderemo i capelli

Se aspettando perderemo i capelli
se la risacca annoderà le gambe
intrise di sale e grinzite di vecchiezza
se fondando caviglie in melma fredda
saremo radici d'inadempienza

velate aspetteremo sulla riva
l'amaro ritorno delle cose perse
finchè le dita diventino lische.
Il mare semina corpi
e germoglia stelle.

(in *Disattese - coro di donne mediterranee*, Versante Ripido, 2019)

Pàrodos

When we're done forgetting of ourselves
and we'll have disappeared completely

only the stones will remain
given back to the stones.
The immortal oaks will stay
in the background of the most solemn white.
The insistent bee buzzing
in the crushing heat.
And black volcano sides that slide into the sea
collapsing from time to time.

(in *Stanze d'isola*, Oèdipus, 2017)

Parodo

Quando avremo finito di dimenticarci di noi stessi
e saremo scomparsi del tutto

resteranno soltanto le pietre
restituite alle pietre.
Resteranno le querce immortali
sullo sfondo del bianco più solenne.
Il ronzio dell'ape insistente
nella calura che schiaccia.
E sciare nere che scivolano in mare
franando, di tanto in tanto.

(in *Stanze d'isola*, Oèdipus, 2017)

Engrave on the high cliff

Engrave on the high cliff
this name of mine
but on any stone so that
may something of me survive
for your fingers, for the harp, for the roar.
Keep it in bands sheltered
within your walls
but lay it down at dawn, in the marly-clay gleam
majestic dazzle on the sea
so that it doesn't add weight to the loom
there, where the languor bit, and the wave
plunges onto the white cliff.

(in *Trittico d'esordio*, edited by A.M. Curci, Cofine, 2017)

Translated from Italian by G. Asmundo and A. Lombardo

Scolpisci sull'alta rupe

Scolpisci sull'alta rupe
questo mio nome
ma su pietra qualunque, così che
possa durare qualcosa di me
alle tue dita, alla lira, al fragore.
Serbala in fasce al riparo
delle tue mura
ma posala all'alba, al lucore marnoso
maestoso abbaglio sul mare
così che non gravi di peso il telaio
là dove morse il languore e l'onda
si getta sull'alta rupe.

(in *Trittico d'esordio*, edited by Anna Maria Curci, Cofine, 2017)

Alessandra Drigo (1994) is a postdoctoral researcher in environmental justice. Growing up in the Venetian countryside, she moved to Venice for her studies. Although Venice always feels like home, she has also lived in St. Petersburg, Berkeley (USA), and in Birmingham (UK). Alessandra's poetry in English follows the duplex structure, following Jericho Brown's formulation.

Alessandra Drigo (1994) è una ricercatrice post-doc in giustizia ambientale. Cresciuta nella campagna veneta, si trasferisce a Venezia per i suoi studi. Nonostante Venezia la senta sempre come casa, ha vissuto anche a San Pietroburgo, Berkeley (USA) Birmingham (Regno Unito). La poesia di Alessandra in inglese segue la struttura del duplex, seguendo la formulazione di Jericho Brown.

The path

Poems don't come quietly to me.
What I bite becomes sticky on my teeth.

Pain always becomes sticky on my teeth,
I'm forced to swear on a last desire: language.

I wasn't forced to swear on my first desire:
to witness the heathland touching my young back.

The heat on the back comes from crowd's shoulders.
Like casual hands reaching your coldest part.

Those hands take me aback, and I lose all sight.
Mild heat on the iris all I wanna see.

Brutal dryness of the iris all I feel.
Poems don't come quietly to me

Il sentiero

Le poesie non mi raggiungono nella quiete.
Ciò che mordo mi si appiccica sui denti.

Il dolore mi si appiccica sempre sui denti,
Sono costretta a giurare su un ultimo desiderio: il linguaggio.

Non sono stata costretta a giurare sul mio primo desiderio:
testimoniare la brughiera che tocca la mia giovanissima
        schiena.

Il calore sulla schiena proviene dalle spalle della folla.
Come casuali mani che raggiungono la vostra parte più fredda.

Quelle mani mi trascinano nell'incertezza e perdo tutta la vista.
Un calore lieve sull'iride, nient'altro voglio vedere.

Una brutale secchezza dell'iride, nient'altro percepisco.
Le poesie non mi raggiungono nella quiete.

Duplex I – Tension

I run in a straight line, hoping to stop.
Ahead of the curve, I forecast an edge.

    The curve becomes a slippery sphere.
    On slippery paths I am left behind.

I'm freefalling behind them, skinny bones.
The trees I climb are always too high,

    I have spoiled hopes that were always too high.
    Large hopes left rusted increase power loss,

Large trajectories increase power loss.
Winds have trajectories that could harm people.

    The wind I carry does not harm people:
    Nor cold nor intertwined with any cloud.

I am not cold nor intertwined with any soul.
I run in a straight line, hoping to stop.

Duplex I – Tensione

Corro in linea retta, sperando di fermarmi.
Davanti alla curva, prevedo un vantaggio.

    La curva diventa una sfera scivolosa.
    Su sentieri scivolosi rimango indietro.

Sono in caduta libera dietro loro, ossa magre.
Gli alberi su cui mi arrampico sono sempre troppo alti,

    Ho stracciato speranze che erano sempre troppo alte.
    Grandi speranze lasciate arrugginire aumentano la
        perdita di potenza,

Traiettorie ampie aumentano la perdita di potenza.
I venti hanno traiettorie che rischiano di danneggiare persone.

    Il vento che trasporto non nuoce alle persone:
    né freddo né intrecciato ad alcuna nuvola.

Non sono fredda né intrecciata con nessuna anima.
Corro in linea retta, sperando di fermarmi.

Duplex II – Swim lesson

Is a force a push or a pull?
Some bellies were a bridge for us to cross.

      Some bellies carry hatred for us to cross.
      Reeds have known to sway for thousands of years.

Drops on rocks for thousands of years left marks.
There are marks on the skin of those who passed that way.

      The way mothers realign bones is universal:
      Within water's weight—solidarity.

We learn to float, making space for our weight.
Our weight's volume rising with the soulful sounds of the
      Blues.

      Our words' volume rising with the soulful sounds of
          the Blues.
      No traveler returns home unchanged.

No survivor ends up as she was before.
A force is a push or a pull.

Duplex II – Lezione di nuoto

Una forza è una spinta o una trazione?
Alcune pance furono per noi un ponte da attraversare.

    Alcune pance ci portano dell'odio da attraversare.
    Le canne sanno come oscillare da migliaia di anni.

Le gocce sulle rocce per migliaia di anni hanno lasciato segni.
Ci sono segni sulla pelle di chi ha passato quella strada.

    Il modo in cui le madri riallineano le ossa è universale:
    All'interno del peso dell'acqua—solidarietà.

Impariamo a galleggiare, facendo spazio al nostro peso.
Il volume del nostro peso aumenta orchestrato ai suoni
    profondi del blues.

    Il volume delle nostre parole aumenta accordato ai
        suoni profondi del blues.
    Nessun viaggiatore fa ritorno così com'era partito.

Nessuna sopravvissuta finisce come era prima.
Una forza è una spinta o una trazione.

Translated from English by A. Lombardo

Giacomo Falchetta is a thirty-year-old who grew up in Venice, a northwestern bend of the Adriatic Sea. Giacomo believes in "creative effort" as an articulation of one's identity. He expresses this effort through his profession as a scientific researcher on issues related to climate change and global poverty, through poetic activity, but also in everyday gestures, such as cooking. Giacomo believes in poetic language as a link between individuals, societies, peoples, and Nature.

Giacomo Falchetta è un trentenne cresciuto a Venezia, ansa nordoccidentale del mare Adriatico. Giacomo crede nello "sforzo creative" come espressione della propria identità. Esprime questo sforzo tramite la propria professione di ricercatore scientifico su tematiche legate al cambiamento climatico e alla povertà globale, tramite l'attività poetica, ma anche nei gesti quotidiani, come cucinare. Giacomo crede nel linguaggio poetico come legame tra le persone, le società, i popoli, e la Natura.

Bond

Even now that the ancient splendor
Of the Sea between the Lands
Is lost for most.

Even now that the blending
And the mysticisms of the sea
You call them folklore.

Even now that Venice,
Damascus, Bizerte
And Piraeus are sad.

An ancient bond
Lives within us. Our fingers
And our tongues float
Like the most beautiful ships

Legame

Anche ora che
Gli antichi fasti
Del Mare tra le Terre
Sono ai più persi.

Anche ora che
Le sincrasie
E i misticismi del mare
Li chiamate folclore.

Anche ora
Che Venezia,
Damasco, Biserta
E il Pireo sono tristi.

Un antico legame
Vive in noi.
Le nostre dita
E le nostre lingue
Le navi più belle.

The ropeyards have closed down

Once a factory of unity
Between light shades
And nested fibres, but now
Reinterpreted by brands
In competition with their own beliefs.

The strings, frayed to the touch,
Remember a hand
Oiled every morning,
Yet exposed to salt
And the air in between.

You perform in ropeyards.
Speak complex words
Talk foreign languages
But I don't understand you.

Go back to tying the jute,
Linen, hemp, and cotton.
Only your human matter
Will reopen the ropeyards.

Le corderie hanno chiuso

Le corderie hanno chiuso.
Opificio dell'unione
Tra sfumature leggere
E fibre arrotolate ma ora
Interpretate con marchi
A vostra detta antitetici.

Al tatto le corde sfibrate
Ricordano una mano
Oliata ogni mattina ma
Troppo esposta al salso
E all'aria dell' in mezzo.

Vi esibite nelle corderie.
Pronunciate parole complesse
In lingue straniere
Ma io non vi capisco.

Tornate a legare juta
Lino, canapa e cotone.
Solo la vostra materia
Riaprirà le corderie.

Dry anthology

Those writing about the sea
Cut through dry waves.
They're just wetter
of the dead calm of the harbour.

But you
Lost Argonauts,
Departed and already forgotten,
And (because missing)
You are soon the past
Do not write
      of the sea
Do not talk
      of diving
Do not sit
      on the edge.

Your weary eyes
Cannot recognize the delicacy
Of mare nostrum
They don't search for horizons
From solitary beaches.

I beg you:
Burn our wet anthology.
With the red lighter you ask
The first passerby
Who isn't intimidated
By your appearance
And request.

Silloge asciutta

Chi scrive di mare
Solca onde asciutte.
Al di più umide
Di bonaccia del porto.

Ma voi
Argonauti persi
Partiti perduti
E (poiché dispersi)
Presto passato
Non scrivete
Di mare
Non parlate
Di tuffi
Non sedete
Sull'orlo.

Le vostre stanche pupille
Non riconoscono dolcezza
Nel mare nostrum
Non cercano orizzonti
Da spiaggie solitarie.

Vi imploro:
Bruciate la nostra silloge umida
Con l'accendino rosso
Del primo passante
Non intimorito
Dal vostro aspetto
E dalla vostra petizione.

The house of the meaning

We will open houses
Accessible to us all
Lost in the compulsive rush
Of the Amazons.

A big red emblem
With red writing
Will stand above
Each entrance:
I produce, for me.

Thus revealing
A new order
In the words and
Hence, in the things.

These houses will be
Bare, naked,
Primitive, virgin.
The intention will be
The only ornament.

A choir of voices
Of the lodgers,
United and laconic,
Will rise to question
"Which product?"

La casa del senso

Apriremo delle case
Accessibili a noi
Tutti smarriti
Nella fretta
Delle Amazzoni.

Un grande cartello
Rosso con una
Scritta rossa
Capeggerà
Ogni accesso:
"ProDuco, pro me".

Palesando
Il nuovo ordine
Delle parole
Dunque, delle cose.

Le case saranno
Spoglie, nude,
Prime, vergini.
L'intento sarà
L'unico ornamento.

Il coro di voci
Degli inquilini
Si solleverà
Unito e laconico:
"Quale prodotto"?

The quest will be
Incessant,
Shared,
        Joyful.

La ricerca sarà
Incessante, condivisa,
     Felice.

The black pines

I read that Cephalonia
Lends its name
To the black pines
Of the Ionian islands.

Indigenous and thriving
They spread an aroma
That is the pepper of the sea-
And the cicadas chirp
Under the dying sun

One day maybe
I'll also be able
To lend my name
To a scented tree.

I pini neri

Ho letto che Cefalonia
Presta il proprio nome
Ai pini neri
Delle isole Jonie.

Autoctoni e rigogliosi
Emanano un aroma
Che è il pepe del mare
E le cicale friniscono
Sotto la fiamma calda.

Forse anche io
Un giorno saprò
Donare il mio nome
A un albero profumato.

Brigidina Gentile has had a fascination with magic and for Penelope since she was a child. First, she worked as a cultural anthropologist in Mexico, where she studied the myths and the magical rituals of the indigenous populations of Chiapas. Then, always under the jaguar sun of that enchanting land she also found Penelope. Today, she weaves as well, using words instead of threads, describing and translating emotions through the mysterious and magical act of writing. See also: www.leteledipenelope.com

Poetry: *Notturni à la carte* (new edition, 2020); *Eros in soffitta e altri ibridi* ["Eros in the Attic and Other Hybrids"] (2018) runner up in the 2018 New York Book Festival; *Kika. La tombola della regina* ["Kika. The Queen's Tombola"] (2020); *Tequila* (2023). Narrative: *Scrivere donna. Letteratura al femminile in America Latina* ["Latin American women literature"] by Brigidina Gentile and Rosa Maria Grillo, translated by Brigidina Gentile (2011); *J'ai fatigué la salade. La vita è come un'insalata* ["I am tired of salad. Life is like a salad."] (2019) a culinary novel that received an Honorable Mention in the London Book Festival 2022; *L'altra Penelope. Tessere il mito* ["The other Penelope. Weaving the myth"] (new edition, 2021) an anthology that was also published in Spanish in 2011 and received an Honorable Mention in the 2012 New York Book Festival. Theater: *Beatrice e lei* ["Beatrice and her"] (2021).

Brigidina Gentile ha avuto fin da bambina una fascinazione per la magia e per Penelope. Ha lavorato prima come antropologa culturale in Messico, dove ha studiato i miti e i riti magici delle popolazioni indigene del Chiapas, e poi sempre sotto il sole giaguaro di questa terra incantevole ha trovato pure Penelope. Oggi tesse anche lei, usando le parole invece dei fili, descrivendo e traducendo emozioni attraverso l'atto misterioso e magico della scrittura. Vedi anche: www.leteledipenelope.com

Poesia: *Notturni à la carte* (n.e. 2020); *Eros in soffitta e altri ibridi* (2018, runner up nel New York Book Festival 2018); *Kika. La tombola della regina* (2020); *Tequila* (2023). Narrativa: *Scrivere donna. Letteratura al femminile in America Latina* (a cura di Brigidina Gentile, Rosa Maria Grillo, traduzione di Brigidina Gentile, 2011); *J'ai fatigué la salade. La vita è come un'insalata* (2019) novella culinaria che ha ricevuto una Honorable Mention nel London Book festival del 2022; *L'altra Penelope. Tessere il mito* (n.e. 2021) antologia che è stata pubblicata anche in spagnolo nel 2011 e che ha ricevuto una Honorable Mention nel New York Book Festival del 2012. Teatro: *Beatrice e lei* (2021).

Basement cleansing

I take away all the twisted words,
the exhausted and sad ones,
of resentment and fear,
even the dead words,
false, out of sync
weak, painful
or without any weight.

I remove also the disused words
along with the indiscreet ones
for a few euros
in a safe mode
and not even a scratch.

Svuota cantine

Porto via tutte le parole storte,
quelle consumate e tristi,
del rancore e della paura,
anche le parole morte,
false, fuori tempo
deboli, dolenti
o senza caratura.

Sgombero pure le desuete
insieme alle parole indiscrete
per pochi euro
in modalità sicura
e nemmeno una graffiatura.

Extrem/ity

My feet feel cold
and I wake up,
the boiler is off
no sound is heard,
the theater of shadows raises the curtain
and on the ceiling the show begins.

I'm afraid
of what's outside,
of the priest inside the confessional,
of the embers in the fireplace,
of being alone.

You sleep next to me
I don't move.

I'm afraid
of waking you up and hearing you scream,
of your hands
that cannot caress but only hit.

Estremi/tà

Sento freddo ai piedi
e mi sveglio,
la caldaia è spenta
non si sente alcun rumore,
il teatro delle ombre apre il sipario
e sul soffitto comincia la funzione.

Ho paura
di quello che c'è fuori,
del prete dentro al confessionale,
delle braci nel camino,
di restare sola.

Tu dormi accanto a me,
io non mi muovo.

Ho paura
di svegliarti e sentirti gridare
delle tue mani
che non sanno fare altro che picchiare.

Menstruation

The playful voices of the children
crowd the courtyard below my house,
it is a burst of life that wakes me up,
but on the border between waking and sleep
you are still there,
little naked merman,
with the sun raining down your hair.

Like Odysseus I watch you vanish
but among the feathers of the pillows,
where I linger a little longer
to feel the viscous warmth
of my month dripping away.

Power of the feminine mystery,
I bleed and I'm more alive than ever,
my breasts are hard and tense, my belly's swollen.

With my fingers I follow my design,
when a question quickly flits through my head:
What if a Tampax were enough to absorb you too?

Mestruazione

Il vociare giocoso dei bimbi
affolla il cortile sotto casa,
uno scoppio di vita che mi sveglia,
ma sul confine tra la veglia e il sonno
ci sei ancora tu,
sirenetto nudo,
con il sole che ti piove nei capelli.

Come Ulisse ti guardo svanire
ma tra le piume dei cuscini
dove indugio un altro poco ancora
per sentire il calore vischioso
del mio mese scivolare.

Potenza del mistero femminile, sanguino
e sono più che mai viva,
i seni duri e tesi, la pancia gonfia.

Con le dita inseguo il mio disegno,
quando in testa rapida mi frulla una domanda:
e se bastasse un Tampax per assorbire anche te?

Differentiated

Words sleep on woolen mattresses
which should be carded and not washed
as instead I did, confident in the future,
while that politician spoke of Pyrrhic victories.

At first, I liked him,
now I prefer garbage men
here they come, punctual,
to collect glass nailed into my heart.

Differenziata

Dormono le parole su vecchi materassi di lana
che andrebbe cardata e non lavata
come ho fatto io fiduciosa nell'avvenire,
mentre quel politico parlava di vittorie di Pirro.

All'inizio mi piaceva,
adesso preferisco gli spazzini,
eccoli puntuali venire a raccogliere i vetri
che ho conficcati sul cuore.

Venetian dream

With the voices of rags,
lace and antique furniture.

In the city of water and marble
lost in her laces
a woman runs
stumbles, falls, gets up again,
remembers
other paths
exact and implacable,
refined threads of fear.

Loneliness is her cloak of feathers.

In the city of water and marbles
she walks the night
but it's the dawn she longs
for under the sheets.

The passing of time is an illusion
the rags say.

Don't be afraid
antique furniture echoes back to her.

In the dormant language of things
she listens to fragments of forgotten voices
and feels the pain turning into anger.

Sogno veneziano

Con le voci degli stracci,
dei merletti e dei mobili antichi.

Nella città d'acqua e di marmi
persa nei suoi merletti
una donna corre
inciampa, cade, si rialza, ricorda
altri sentieri esatti, implacabili,
raffinati fili di paura.

La solitudine è il suo manto di piume.

Nella città d'acqua e marmi
cammina la notte
ma è l'alba che anela
sotto alle lenzuola.

Lo scorrere del tempo è
un'illusione
dicono gli stracci.

Non temere
le fanno eco i mobili
antichi.

Nella lingua addormentata
delle cose frammenti di voci dimenticate
ascolta e sente il dolore farsi rabbia.

Please, stop the shadow of her sleepless feet!
In the geography of darkness
they follow and chase the rhythm of wood
the streets of Venice whisper,
while the night gives way to the light
and easy breathing of vaporetti.

The Grand Canal swallows
carcasses and desires, even ghosts
among fog and waves.

Behind the still closed shutters
the woman sleeps
embraced to the warmth of a man
who will never know her.

(From *Tequila. Spirit's infused poetry* (2024)
Translation by Brigidina Gentile)

Fermate l'ombra dei suoi piedi insonni!
Nella geografia del buio
inseguono il ritmo del legno
mormorano le calli
mentre la notte cede il passo
alla respirazione leggera e facile dei vaporetti.

Il Canal Grande inghiotte
desideri e carcasse, anche
fantasmi tra nebbia e onde.

Dietro le persiane ancora chiuse
la donna dorme
abbracciata al calore di un uomo
che non la saprà mai.

Fabia Ghenzovich was born in Venice, where she currently lives. She is interested in poetry and its possible interactions and cross-pollination between the languages of art and music, as she did in her rap poem collection *Metropoli*, as well as in the cross-pollination between language and dialect.

Some of her poems have been translated into Romanian in *Tribuna Magazin* (Romanian magazine of Italian poetry); some of her haikus illustrated by painters and graphic designers and translated into Russian by the poet and critic Pavel Aleshin in a Russian magazine. Other lyrics translated into English by Pina Piccolo. She has won the following prizes in poetry competitions: Guido Gozzano in 2009, the Charles Darwin Scientific Poetry Prize in 2014, the Anna Osti Prize in 2016, the Mazzavillani Prize for Italian dialects in 2020 and the first prize for poetry published in dialect Pinwheel of Words in 2021.

Published Books: *Giro di boa* (Joker, 2007); *Il cielo aperto del corpo* (Kolibris, 2011 and in paperback and in ebook on LaRecherche.it, 2016); *Totem* (punto a capo Editrice, 2015); *Se ti la vardi contra luse* (Supernova, 2018) first book in Venetian dialect; *Nudità* (Il Leggio, 2020); *Haiku* (Centro Internazionale della Grafica, 2022) published in Venetian dialect with images by artists in dialogue with her poems.

Fabia Ghenzovich è nata a Venezia, dove vive. Esplora le interazioni e le contaminazioni tra il linguaggio poetico e la musica (come appare nella sua poesia rap *Metropoli*) così come tra lingua e dialetto.

Ha pubblicato sei libri di poesie. Alcune sue poesie sono state tradotte in rumeno sulla *Tribuna Magazin* (rivista rumena di poesia italiana); alcuni dei suoi haiku, illustrati da pittori, tradotti in russo dal poeta e critico Pavel Aleshin; altri testi sono stati tradotti in inglese da Pina Piccolo e Anna Lombardo. Ha vinto i seguenti premi in concorsi di poesia: Guido Gozzano nel 2009, Premio Poesia Scientifica Charles Darwin nel 2014, Premio Anna Osti nel 2016, Premio Mazzavillani per i dialetti italiani nel 2020, e il primo premio per la poesia pubblicata in dialetto Girandola di Parole nel 2021.

Libri pubblicati: *Giro di boa* (edizioni Joker, 2007); *Il cielo aperto del corpo* (edizioni Kolibris, 2011 in brossura e in ebook su La Recherche, 2016); *Totem* (Puntoacapo Editrice, 2015); *Se ti la vardi contra luse* (edizioni Supernova, 2018) primo libro in dialetto veneto; *Nudità* (Il Leggio, 2020); *Haiku* (dialetto veneziano con immagini di artisti in dialogo con le sue poesie) edito dal Centro Internazionale Veneziano di Grafica Venezia, 2022. È inoltre membro del comitato artistico del Festival Internazionale di Poesia "Palabra en el Mundo" per Venezia.

Where everything ends

the cry goes up
the hands raised to the sky
and on the eyes to cover
the dismay.

Where everything ends
rubble and bodies
sing the darkest note
of mourning that the cosmos
collects.

Tears are not enough
to wash the wound in the dark
where we had already been

descendants of Cain.
Jewish, Christian, or Muslim
your name is murderer, not man
anymore.

Dove tutto finisce

s'alza il grido
mani levate al cielo
sugli occhi per coprire
lo spavento.

Dove tutto finisce
macerie e corpi
cantano la nota più cupa
che il cosmo raccoglie
del lutto.

Non bastano lacrime
a lavare la ferita nel buio
dove eravamo già stati

discendenti di Caino
ebreo, cristiano, o mussulmano
ti chiami assassino non più
uomo.

It's happened for real

out of blue, the light has slipped
away. I don't know where it went
and like with Peter Pan from under
his feet—but upside down—there was
the shadow. A heads and tails
with the invisible!

Declaring my love
it was useless, not even
a glimpse comes around
a sign of hope
to be able to peak at it,
the light. Deliberately, instead,
the shadow becomes

bright and with the other
partner twin, it teases like with a rat,
a cat that,
they say,

in the almond-shaped gap
of his eyes, the infinite
is hidden, where nobody reaches.

È accaduto davvero

mi si è sfilata di punto in bianco
la luce. Non so dove si sia
cacciata come a Peter Pan
da sotto i piedi - ma al contrario -
l'ombra. Un testa e croce
con l'invisibile!

Dichiararle il mio amore
è stato inutile nemmeno
una stilla si è fatta avanti
un minimo spiraglio
per poterla sbirciare
la luce invece a farlo apposta
mi si illumina

l'ombra che a turno con l'altra
complice gemella
stuzzica come col topo
un gatto che
dicono

degli occhi nella fessura
a mandorla nasconda
l'infinito dove nessuno giunge.

One day in Venice

It would be enough this double-light,
that is mirrored and bounces
on the water exactly
like the sounds and the voices
of those who live in Venice.
A constant chatter
of waves that blend with the chant
of the dialect with the gibberish of the steps
but without haste and it stays

right into the depths of the beauty
an apparent peace that has no time
as if eternity could be measured
       in the light.
It would just be enough to stop
to say life is here now
between coming and going
without asking anything
nothing more to understand
just this feeling
being here   being ready

       for oblivion.

Un giorno a Venezia

Basterebbe questa luce doppia
che si specchia e rimbalza
sull'acqua esattamente
come i suoni e le voci
di chi a Venezia vive.
Un chiacchiericcio continuo
di onde si fonde con la cantilena
del dialetto col borbottio dei passi
ma senza fretta sosta

fin dentro ai meandri della bellezza
una pace tersa che non ha tempo
come se si potesse misurare l'eternità
    nella luce.
Basterebbe solo fermarsi
per dire la vita è qui adesso
tra il venire e l'andare
senza nulla chiedere
niente più da capire
soltanto questo sentirsi
esserci   essere pronti

   all'oblio.

Not everything changes

Not everything changes
under layers and layers
moods simply urge.
A magma
of shocks and denials
so as not to remember that useless
digging of burrows,
of pits.

Neutral yesterday caves in now
it disappears to come back
like the good and the evil

thus, in every story
the flame (burning)
falls in the end.

Maybe a heartbeat
an echo of drums

on sacred ground
a dancing woman.

Non tutto muta

Non tutto muta
semplicemente sotto strati e strati
premono umori.
Un magma
di scosse e rimozioni
per non ricordare quell'inutile
scavare di tane
di fosse.

Ieri neutrale cede adesso
scompare per tornare
così il bene e il male

così di ogni storia
la fiammella (ardendo)
alla fine cade.

Forse un battito
una eco di tamburi

su terra sacra
una donna che danza.

One step after another

that would be too simple
a climb without the tension
that tests you
the hurdle of a need
lurking too easy

to avoid a fiasco
call each other brothers in the rift
in the cut with the bitterness
of a smile ever
quite torn.

Give me an ordinary
darkness, transcend me
the prey in the triumph
of a mask blasphemous over
the centuries of the centuries, search for me
the directionless compass

freedom comes naked.*

homage to ChlebniKov

Uno scalino dopo l'altro

sarebbe troppo semplice
una salita senza la tensione
che ti metta alla prova
l'inciampo di un bisogno
in agguato troppo facile

sventare un fiasco
dirsi fratelli nello strappo
nel taglio con l'amaro
di un sorriso mai
abbastanza dilaniato.

Datemi pure una tenebra
abituale trascendetemi
la preda nel trionfo
di una maschera nei secoli
dei secoli blasfema cercatemi
la bussola senza direzione

*la libertà arriva nuda.**

(omaggio ChlebniKov))

Alessandra Pellizzari was born in Verona and lives in Venice. She is an art historian and teacher.

Publication poetry collections: *Lettere a cera persa* (Lietocolle, 2006) with preface by Andrea Zanzotto; *Intermittenze*, artist's book with a score by Saverio Tasca; *Mutamenti* (Campanotto, 2012); *Faglie* (Puntoacapo, 2017) preface by Elio Grasso; *Nodi parlati-Clove Hitches, a Venice poem*, (NEM, 2009) translation by Patrick Williamson; *Venetia: noduri cabestan* (Editura Cosmopoli, 2023) translated by Eliza Macadan. She is also present in the anthology *12 Poetesse italiane* (NEM, 2007).

In 2019 she published a children's book: *SOS Venezia e la laguna! Filastrocche di Otto il bassotto*, illustrated by the children participating in the drawing and painting atelier of the Martin Egge Onlus Foundation in Venice.

Her poems have been translated into English, French, and Romanian and are in anthologies, magazines, and blogs.

Alessandra Pellizzari è nata a Verona e vive a Venezia; storica dell'arte e insegnante.

Pubblicazioni: Lettere a cera persa (Lietocolle 2006) con prefazione di Andrea Zanzotto; Intermittenze, libro d'artista con una partitura di Saverio Tasca; 12 testi per l'antologia 12 poetesse italiane (NEM, 2007) con testo critico di Francesco Carbognin; Mutamenti (Campanotto, 2012) Faglie (Puntoacapo 2017) prefazione di Elio Grasso; Nodi parlati-Clove Hitches, a Venice poem (NEM, 2009) traduzione di Patrick Williamson; Venetia: noduri cabestan (Editura Cosmopoli, 2023) traduzione di Eliza Macadan.

Nel 2019 ha pubblicato un libro per bambini: S.O.S. Venezia e la laguna, filastrocche di Otto il bassotto, illustrato dai ragazzi partecipanti all'atelier di disegno e pittura della Fondazione Martin Egge Onlus di Venezia.

Le sue poesie sono tradotte in inglese, francese e romeno, sono presenti in antologie, riviste e blog.

Poetry from **Nodi parlati-Clove Hitches, a Venice poem**, NEM 2009

Translation by Patrick Williamson and Alessandra Pellizzari

Voices sing on the roofs of preludes,
through foggy caves of archivolts,
whenever wandering violins
are silenced.

Where will the contaminated beauty end?
Perhaps, on a more serious note,
with the misunderstood gesture of a belfry,
on the undulating fraction of time?
Over there,
where migratory birds leave
the dicey dwellings of a suffocated arch,
among the encrypted smudges of a ship.
Perhaps on the sandy wind,
on the dark truths of silt?
When the sharp truths
of Istrian stone
give way to the evidence of rust seaweed,
on brick-bones,
garnet red,
skinned by powders,
vanish into the Gothic enclosure,
silences snarled.

Poesie da: *Nodi parlati-Clove Hitches, a Venice poem*, NEM 2009

Quando sulle coperture dei preludi
si zittiscono i violini girovaghi,
gli antri annebbiati degli archivolti,
intonano voci.

Dove finirà la contaminata bellezza?
Forse su una voce più grave,
sul gesto incompreso
di una cella campanaria,
sull'ondulata frazione di tempo?
Laggiù,
dove gli uccelli migratori lasciano
le dimore incerte dell'arco soffocato,
tra le sbavature cifrate di una nave.
Forse sul vento sabbioso,
sulle fosche verità delle seti?
Quando le taglienti verità
della pietra d'Istria,
cederanno all'evidenza dell'algosa ruggine,
sulle lische dei mattoni,
il rosso granata,
scorticato dalle polveri,
andrà a svanire nella chiusa gotica,
annodando i silenzi.

How do you describe the colour purple?
It was once the semblance of flesh,
on the cinnabar stitches of stars.
It was the melody of marine silence,
on the door to the earth. On the door
where the winged lion guards
the tower of masts,
among tormented cornices of scarlet maple,
the recitatives of claws,
strands of dew from the east.

When the features turn
towards skies of pain,
they will distill fugues of marble, from lips,
under the guidance of a sunset.
And the great waterway breaks forth
from a major note,
the harmonious cacophony of the sacred ibis.
Will the color of blood be able to say?
Will the unusual light shine? Before the sun stirs, the gurgle of
hoods will climb again
through screeching masks and clusters of Byzantine crosses,
over the abyss of voids,
on the last act of courtly reflexes.

How will the colour purple be able to tell?

Come dire il colore imporporato?
Era un tempo il sembiante della carne,
sui magli cinabri delle stelle.
Era la melodia del silenzio marino,
sulla porta di terra. Sulla porta
dove il leone alato sorveglia la torre
di alberatura,
tra le tormentate cornici d'acero rosso,
i recitativi di artigli,
i filamenti della rugiada d'oriente.

Quando i lineamenti volgeranno
verso i cieli del dolore,
distilleranno dalle labbra, le fughe del marmo,
sulle direttrici di un tramonto.
Da una nota maggiore,
la grande strada d'acqua sferzerà
le armoniose cacofonie dell'ibis sacro.
Potrà il colore del sangue dire?
Splenderà l'insolita luce? Prima che il sole
si risvegli, sugli abissi dei vuoti,
sull'ultimo atto dei riflessi cortesi,
i gorgoglii delle cappe risaliranno
tra gli stridori dei mascheroni e i viluppi di croci bizantine.

Come potrà il colore imporporato dire?

Cormorants about to leave
the lace of sandbanks,
while seagulls frame the dawn.
Footsteps echoing the streets, ruffled
leaves crackling
on the trails of thunderstruck skies,
buried among memories in the mud.
Hands, reflections, earth-covered bodies,
among bare scrub and sheets of seaweed,
music motifs, meetings of salt mouths
greedy for sounds.

Dai merletti delle barene
i cormorani si apprestano a partire,
mentre i gabbiani incorniciano l'alba.
Il rumore dei passi tra le calli, il crepitio
di foglie increspate
sulle scie dei cieli stralunati,
s'insabbiano tra i ricordi nel fango.
Le mani, i riflessi, i corpi terrosi,
tra gli sterposi nulla e i fogli d'alga,
i motivi di musiche, gli incontri di sale
le bocche avide di suoni.

Will uncertain transparency on hollow gray sentences
be able to accompany me?
Through the cracks of ashlar?
On phrases shackled to the centrality of graphism,
to bottlenecks of time,
to the bridges, the modesty of the canals, the chiseled slopes,
and gutted rii,
the intertwining of the full and empty spaces of
networks? There, where illuminated wakes
and spiced papers survive, there,
where algae-green rests on the slight summit,
there, where the black quietens.

Sarà capace di accompagnarmi la trasparenza incerta
sulle frasi incavate di grigio?
Attraverso le fessure del bugnato?
Sulle frasi incatenate alla centralità di grafismi,
alle strettoie del tempo,
ai ponti, ai pudori dei canali, alle falde cesellate,
agli sventrati rii,
sugli intrecci dei pieni e dei vuoti delle reti?
Lì, dove sopravvivono i solchi miniati,
le carte speziate, lì
dove il verdealga riposa sulla cima leggera,
lì, dove il nero s'acquieta.

Adam Vaccaro was born in Bonefro, Molise in 1940, and lives in Milan.

He is a poet and critic and has published about 20 books, including poetry collections and essays on art and poetry. Among his published poetry collections there are: *La casa sospesa* ["The house suspended"] (Joker, 2003); *La piuma e l'artiglio* ["Feather and claw"] (Editoria e Spettacolo, Rome 2006); *Seeds: Selected Poems 1978-2006* (Chelsea Editions, New York, 2014,); *Tra lampi e corti* ["Between flashes and shorts"] (Marco Saya, Milan 2019); *Identità bonefrana. Poesia tra radici e visioni* (Di Felice Edizioni, 2020); *Il nome di Dio. In quattro quarti di cuore* (Collezione Letteraria, 2021); *In respiratia zilei* ["In the breath of the day"] translated by Alexandru Macadan, (Editura Cosmopoli, Bacau, Romania, 2023).

As a critic and essayist, he collaborates with magazines and newspapers. He has received many awards and has been translated into Spanish, English and Romanian.

He is a founder and the president of cultural association Milanocosa since 2000. He promoted the following events: "Poetry in action," "Poetic Bunker," at the 49th Venice Art Biennale 2001; "Scriptures/Reality – Comparing languages and disciplines," 2003; "7 words from the contemporary world," 2005; "Milan: History and Imagination," 2011; *The gardener against the gravedigger*, (conference on Antonio Porta and publication of the acts of the conference, 2009 – 2012).

He is included in the *Atlas of Contemporary Poetry* edited by the University of Bologna, as well as in many blogs and anthological collections. He edits the online cultural magazine *Adiacenze;* and together with Giuliano Zosi and other musicians he organized concerts of music and poetry.

Adam Vaccaro è nato a Bonefro, Molise, nel 1940, e vive a Milano.

È poeta e critico e ha pubblicato circa 20 libri, tra raccolte di poesie e saggi sull'arte e sulla poesia. Tra le sue raccolte di poesie pubblicate si ricordano: *La casa sospesa*, (Novi Ligure 2003); *La piuma e l'artiglio*, (Editoria & Spettacolo, Roma 2006); *Semi, semi*, (New York 2014, Chelsea Editions); *Tra Lampi e Corti*, (Saya Ed, Milano 2019); *Identità Bonefrana*, (Felice Edizioni, Martinsicuro 2020); *Google – il nome di Dio*, (Puntoacapo Editrice, Pasturana, 2021); *In respiratia zilei (Nel respiro del giorno)* tradotto da Alexandru Macadan, (Editura Cosmopoli, Bacau, Romania, 2023).

Come critico e saggista, collabora con riviste e giornali. Ha ricevuto numerosi premi ed è stato tradotto in spagnolo, inglese e rumeno.

È fondatore e presidente dell'associazione culturale Milanocosa dal 2000. Ha promosso le seguenti manifestazioni: "Poesia in azione", "Bunker Poetico", alla 49° Biennale d'Arte di Venezia 2001; "Scritture/Realtà – Linguaggi e discipline a confronto", 2003; "7 parole dal mondo contemporaneo", 2005; "Milano: Storia e Immaginazione", 2011; *Il giardiniere contro il becchino*, (convegno su Antonio Porta e pubblicazione degli atti del convegno, 2009 – 2012).

È presente nell'Atlante della poesia contemporanea curato dall'Università di Bologna, oltre che in numerosi blog e raccolte antologiche. Dirige la rivista culturale online *Adiacenze*; e insieme a Giuliano Zosi e ad altri musicisti organizzò concerti di musica e poesia.

Images

Images of white and light
on wings sturdy in flesh
that return once more to our
first source of life preserved
as sunlit fields of white snow
blanket desire for the present
and the promise of a future life
"under snow the grain grows" (1)
To you, fields, I leave this solo
for a land that still stubbornly seeks
new fathers somewhere between
the Proci suitors and these closed stones
with crazed Ulysses and a thousand black
Penelopes—wise to the lightning and
songs, the deeds and tales of a love

untamed—as they keep on growing seeds.

*

Immagini

immagini di bianco e luce
su ali resistenti nella carne
che riportano alla prima
fonte mai perduta di vita
campi di neve al sole che
una coperta ponevano tra
fame del presente e futuro
promessa sotto la neve pane (1)
affido a voi l'assolo di questa
terra che cerca ancora testarda
rinnovati padri e madri al croce
via tra questi sassi chiusi e proci
con folli Ulisse e mille Penelopi
nere che sanno i lampi e canti
i riti e miti d'amore indomiti

che coltivano ancora semi

The Necessary Knife

Immense, the lunar spectacle
circled by unflinching life
sniffs feeble and unyielding
like a bear pierced to the heart
But it would make most sense
to start again from you, and coast
along on the brink of horror
with a daily spoonful of honey.
Love—he only knife necessary
to make of horror an open belly.

*

Coltello necessario

Immenso spettacolo e lunare
accerchiato da una vita accanita
che sguarnita e inarresa annusa
come un orso ferito
al cuore
ma conviene ripartire da te
da questa punta di miele la mattina
per viaggiare lungo gli orli
dell'orrore. Amore
unico coltello necessario
a fare dell'orrore un ventre aperto

(In: *La piuma e l'artiglio*, Roma 2006)

Fifth Courtyard (2)

Milan threads its subway tunnels
chasing brisk instants that added
up amount to nothing
to turn them into heaps of rubble
between dreams of lost green
and enchanted September meetings
where sausages are singed black and red flags
wave, parentheses wait for kids with a knack
for playing the dating game with a syringe;
Milan now impales its mangled dreams
on wise skewers roasting piles of cash,
riches spared all aches and cares
and yet Milan still spears one courtyard to the next
finding time in the end, before it disappears.

*

Quintocortile

Milano infila tunnel del metrò
per rincorse di istanti veloci
che sommati fanno un niente
per farne montagne di macerie
tra sogni di un perduto verde e
incanti di incontri che a settembre
fumavano salsicce e bandiere rosse
parentesi in attesa di ragazzi bravi
a fare il gioco delle coppie con siringa
Milano ora fila sogni disfatti su uno spiedo
sapiente che cucina mucchi di denari
ricchezze povere di dolori e pensieri
Milano infila eppure ancora cortili uno dentro l'altro
che ritrovano in fondo – ancora visibile – il tempo

(In *La piuma e l'artiglio*, Roma 2006)

Juice

At times, the juice of this life
—once it has crossed the rickety,
radiant gap—tries to translate
it all, front and back, into words
that taste of sugar and salt, within
and without—so sweet they leave
us in a daze, so salty they crack
our lips in the desert's gale
that pushes us on without fail.

*

Il succo

Il succo di questo nostro esistere
che tenta a volte slabbrato
il salto sgangherato e fulgido
di tradurre tutto
il suo dritto e il suo rovescio
in parole dal sapore
di zucchero e sale
completamente dentro e
completamente fuori—così
dolce da stordirci e
salato da spaccare le labbra
nel vento del deserto
che spinge senza tregua
a proseguire

(30 dicembre 2009)

Memories of the Future

The ashes of Auschwitz's smoke
so white at first, and then purple and red
beat hard in the heart like a roach
that will never fly, destined instead
to gnaw amid these wrecks
feeding insatiably, and without rest
on our boundless black blood,
guzzling all blood and every victim
turned to ash and placed in the hands
of Ceres, bearing testimony
to an Earth no longer prone to powers
and insanities present and bygone
an Earth that knows how to weigh
every pound of human flesh, first
red, then purple and white,
on the very same scale
offered up to the god of all
people and worlds, rich
and poor, knowing no
privilege or sons chosen
by an Earth that has ceased to be
crucified by borders and banquets
lavishly decked out by the elect
and besieged by heaps of roaches,
starved and insane—
If this is a man.

(from: *Seeds*, Chelsea Editions, New York, 2014)

Memorie del futuro

La cenere dei fumi di Auschwitz
così bianca, viola infine rossa
batte batte dentro al cuore
non volerà ricadrà su questi
ruderi e cori di blatte
a nutrire il nostro sangue
acceso che pesa ogni grammo
di carne umana
rossa poi viola infine bianca
di ogni vittima diventata cenere
deposta nelle mani di Cerere-che
ne faccia messi di una Terra
non più prona a poteri e follie
offerta al dio di tutti
senza figli prediletti
di una Terra non più
crocifissa da confini e
tavole imbandite di eletti
assediate da cumuli di blatte
affamate impazzite-
se questo è un uomo

(2005 – in Antologie varie e in *Seeds*, New York, 2014)

Notes: 1) *under the snow there lies bread*, is a Molisan saying.

2) The Fifth Courtyard is the name of a contemporary art gallery in Milan.

Note: 1) *Sotto la neve pane*, è un proverbio molisano.

2) Quintocortile è il nome di una galleria d'arte contemporanea di Milano.

Valeria Raimondi is one of the founders of the Underground Movement Association (in 2015) which deals with dissemination and research in the poetic field.

Books: *Io no(ex-io)*, 2011 Thauma; *Debito il tempo*, Fusibilia-Pellicano ed., 2014; 2021 *Il penultimo giorno*, Fara edition, 2021; *Io no(ex-io)*, Puntoacapo ed. (revised and re-edited), 2023.

Her poems appear in: *Poetree*, a bilingual Italian-Albanian anthology for three voices (Beppe Costa, Jack Hirschman, and Valeria Raimondi), 2016; *Uma poetry hoie*, a bilingual Italian-Portuguese anthology, 2018.

Some of her "invectives" are included in the Journal of the Departments of the Collage de 'Pataphysique.

She designed and edited the anthology, *Our buried class - Poetic chronicles from the worlds of work*, Pietre Vive Edition, 2019. In 2020 her articles on the pandemic in the region of Lombardy, Italy, were published in Carmilla blog and *Micromega* magazine.

In 2021 she contributed to the application of the Bacchelli Law for the Italian poet Beppe Costa.

Valeria Raimondi: è tra i fondatori dell'Associazione Movimento Underground (nel 2015) che si occupa di divulgazione e ricerca in ambito poetico.

Libri: *Io no(ex-io)*, 2011 Thauma; *Debito il tempo*, Fusibilia-Pellicano ed., 2014; 2021 *Il penultimo giorno*, edizione Fara, 2021; *Io no(ex-io)*, Puntoacapo ed. (rivisto e rieditato), 2023.

Le sue poesie compaiono in: *Poetree*, antologia bilingue italiano-albanese a tre voci (Beppe Costa, Jack Hirschman e Valeria Raimondi), 2016; *Uma poetry hoie*, antologia bilingue italiano-portoghese, 2018.

Alcune sue "invettive" sono inserite nel Giornale dei Dipartimenti del Collegio di Patafisica.

Ha ideato e curato l'antologia *La nostra classe sepolta - Cronache poetiche dai mondi del lavoro*, Edizione Pietre Vive, 2019. Nel 2020 i suoi articoli sulla pandemia in Lombardia, Italia, sono stati pubblicati sul blog Carmilla e sulla rivista "Micromega".

Nel 2021 ha contribuito all'applicazione della Legge Bacchelli per il poeta italiano Beppe Costa.

Po Valley, March 2020

A road is lost between wheat and ditches
sparse rows of knotty mulberries and *leafless* banks
not by nature but by human hands
which flattens the curved line of the plain.

From here, you can't see the freedom
of the grass, the bustle of the worms
the mole's tenacious and gasping work
the robbed partridge's nest

you don't know when the apparent sleep of the earth comes
when it crosses the straight line, the horizon

because the presence doesn't spend words
the light does not ask for distance
no leaves are stirred in the narrow space
of my eyes, captured by the enchantment in the foliage.

Pianura padana, marzo 2020

Una strada si perde tra grano e fossi
radi filari di nodosi gelsi e rive *sfronde*
non per natura ma per mano d'uomo
che *atterra* la linea curva della piana.

Da qui non scorgi la libertà
dell'erba, il tramestio dei vermi
il lavorio tenace, affannato della talpa
il nido rapinato della starna

non sai quando giunge il sonno apparente della terra
quando valica la retta, l'orizzonte

poiché non spende parole la presenza
luce non chiede la distanza
non s'agitano foglie alla fessura stretta
dei miei occhi, rapiti dall'incanto tra le fronde.

Memory

Not like seed pushed away
rather like ash
you germinate lands beyond your hard borders
before and after the going of the people.

You watch for a sign
raise your arms to the sky
and wings of big toes twisted down
further down
between the roots and the humus
in the mercy of the dark
where worms get bread
the atrophied bronchi oxygen.
Sounds of breaking shells,
Cadences are memories
that stubbornly last
beyond the deeds without narrators
beyond the news without witnesses,
open wounds that don't ask
to free oneself in tears
to *repair*.

This is your fair indifference
where everything is lost
but it asks to be defended
from our sorrowful
distracted *care*.

Memoria

Non come seme spinto via
piuttosto come cenere
germini terre oltre i tuoi confini
duri prima e dopo il corso delle genti.

Sorvegli un segno
spingi le braccia al cielo
e ali di alluci contorti giù
più giù
tra le radici e l'humus
nella pietà del buio
dove ottengono pane i vermi
ossigeno i bronchi atrofizzati.
Rumori di gusci rotti
Cadenze sono le memorie
che ostinate durano
oltre le gesta senza narratori
oltre le cronache senza testimoni
ferite aperte che non chiedono
di liberarsi in pianto
di *riparare*.

Questa la tua equa indifferenza
dove tutto si disperde
ma chiede di essere difeso
dal nostro doloso
distratto *incustodire*.

The word is now ex-hausted

The word is now ex-hausted
it comes late as a shadow over things
spoken or written it carries inside its decline
it already reveals the languor, from the morning.

The *verb* changes during the night, it becomes mute
like a mutineer lowers its sails
white is the hand that flies and is already in the shadow
immediately dissolves into foam, the wave.

And the idea, powerful scream, that simply wants
to reveal *the true, the right, the good,*
seems a sigh down the neck of the *already-said*
a breath that the mirror barely clouds over.

La parola è ormai sfinita

La parola è ormai (s)finita
giunge tardi come ombra sulle cose
detta o scritta porta dentro il suo declino
già rivela il languore, dal mattino.

Muta il *verbo* nella notte, ammutolisce
ammutinato ammaina le sue vele
bianca sventola la mano e già s'adombra
si *sfa* subitamente in schiuma, l'onda.

E l'Idea potente urlo che vorrebbe
rivelare solo *il vero, il giusto, il buono*
pare fiato sopra il collo del *già detto*
un respiro che lo specchio appena appanna.

Generation

Sometimes I hide in my sleep
in the moist preparation of the crops
and there you come to find me again
and name my sorrows one by one.
But if you leave, it is me who hopes
the grace of the miracle will renew:
to watch the children growing up,
the leaves falling,
and the substance springing up,

though we know of the shattering of bones and earth,
the eternal indifference of the waters,
the necessary extinction of every species.

But yet, it doesn't end the game of finding each other,
of brooding eggs of others in the mirrors
to generate a seed to be fully nourished
                        —a desire
in the push that then implodes
at the first beat of the morning light.
It is you coming back to shore again
to remind me we are nothing
but in that wave, something still persists,
something like a creation.

(Translated by Cristina Gozzoli)

Generazione

Talvolta mi nascondo dentro il sonno
nell'umida gestazione dei raccolti
e lì, sei tu che vieni ad incontrarmi
per nominare uno ad uno i miei dolori.
Ma se ti assenti, sono io che spero
si rinnovi la grazia del miracolo:
vedere crescere i figli,
cadere le foglie,
generarsi la materia,

sebbene si sappia lo sbriciolarsi delle ossa
e della terra,
l'indifferenza eterna delle acque,
l'estinzione necessaria di ogni specie.

Ma non finisce ancora il gioco di cercarsi,
di covare uova d'altre negli specchi
per generare un seme tutto da nutrire:
                    -un desiderio
nella spinta che poi implode
al primo battito di luce del mattino.
Sei tu che ancora torni a riva
a rammentarmi che non siamo niente
ma che in quell'onda tuttavia perdura qualcosa,
qualcosa che somiglia a una creazione.

Zingonia Zingone is a graduate in Economics, a poet, a novelist, and a translator who writes in Spanish, Italian, French and English. Her poetry books are published in Spain, Mexico, Colombia, Nicaragua, Costa Rica, Italy, France, and India. Her collected poems were printed in Colombia in 2019: *El canto de la sulamita / Songs of the Shulammite* (Colección Anverso, Uniediciones). Her books in English are available in India at Paperwall Media & Publishing: https://paperwall.in and in Colombia at Uniediciones: info@grupoeditorialibanez.com. She is the founder of FreeFromChains poetry workshops and an editorial advisor of Mexican literary magazine *El Golem*.

Zingonia Zingone- è laureata in Economia, poetessa, scrittrice e traduttrice che scrive in spagnolo, italiano, francese e inglese. I suoi libri sono pubblicati in Spagna, Messico, Colombia, Nicaragua, Costa Rica, Italia, Francia e India. La sua raccolta di poesie è stata stampata in Colombia nel 2019: *El canto de la sulamita / Songs of the Shulammite* (Colección Anverso, Uniediciones). I suoi libri in inglese sono disponibili in India presso Paperwall Media & Publishing: https://paperwall.in e Colombia presso Uniediciones: info@grupoeditorialibanez.com. È fondatrice dei laboratori di poesia FreeFromChains e consulente editoriale della rivista letteraria messicana *El Golem*.

Poetry from *Light, the Temptation/ Le tentazioni della Luce*

      Calf's eyes
Evoke distant times
When man was branch
Of the only tree
And the tree lived unhindered
In timeless space

Those eyes watch me
Crossing the field
Observe each move
The abusive current that gushes
From man

I hasten my pace
The calf retreats
It knows
We are siblings
It knows
About Cain and Abel

Poesie da *Le tentazioni della Luce*

gli occhi del vitello
evocano tempi lontani
quando l'uomo era un ramo
dello stesso albero
e l'albero viveva senza tormento

mi osservano
mentre attraverso il campo
scrutano ogni movimento
nella corrente iniqua
che dall'uomo erompe

accelero il passo
e il vitello retrocede
sa
che siamo fratelli
sa
di Caino e Abele

In India
Dogs are nomads
Pace the dusty
Chaotic streets
They know the way
To the end of all roads

A young Palestinian
Looking out of the bus window
Asks
"Where do dogs go?
Dogs are always going…"
He takes my hand
Shuts in the grip of dawn
A ruthless memory
Children
Their empty glances
Licked
By dogs of hate
And mothers of his land
Torn from the good
Crying
Discovering
That all alleys
Are blind

In India
i cani sono nomadi
camminano per le strade
polverose e sconnesse
sanno
dove portano le vie

un giovane palestinese guarda
dal finestrino dell'auto
e domanda
«ma dove vanno i cani?
i cani vanno, vanno…»
prende la mia mano
                    chiude
nel pugno dell'alba
lo spietato ricordo

i bambini
dallo sguardo vuoto
lambiti dai cani dell'odio
e le madri della sua terra
strappate al bene
gemendo
scoprono vicoli ciechi.

The poet opens way
Towards Nizamuddin's tomb
Barefoot
Crosses the bazaar
Dirt
Rubbish
Deformed bodies

He buys flowers
Whistles a Persian tune
Prepares inner silence
To welcome divine inspiration

I follow him overtly
Deep within
The crazed flock
Lost of the good shepherd

We step on marble
Over spits and crushed shells
Poverty's splendor

Il poeta
si fa strada
cerca
la tomba di Nizamuddin
attraversa scalzo
il bazar
il lerciume
i corpi sfigurati

compra fiori
fischia una melodia persiana
prepara
il silenzio interiore che accoglie
la divina ispirazione

lo seguo
incautamente penetro
il gregge impazzito
che ha perso il buon pastore

calpestiamo il marmo
gli sputi
le bucce maciullate
la povertà in tutto il suo splendore

In front of the mausoleum
The poet prays
To the saint of another God
Declares his love of neighbor

Dragging himself
A maimed man follows us
Begging
For a shred of smile
A coin of communion

di fronte al mausoleo
il poeta prega il santo
di un altro dio
dichiara
il suo amore per il prossimo

il mutilato trascinandosi ci insegue
chiede
una briciola di sorriso
gli spiccioli
di questa comunione.

The Beginning of Birth Pains

The last partition falls
Down on Fall's remains

Torn, children continue
Jumping the rope
—an old rolled sheet—
As a doctor mends the wounded
Blanket between drainage stains

As strong as death
Is mothers' love
Giving light
To pain's trace

The tile has fallen
Exploding in the air
Crowning the soil
Joining edges of a ditch
Sheltering the pretty Syrian rose
Asleep on her bed of blood

Rise, love,
From the debris
Rise below the glancing sky
Its love begets, thus
Rise

L'Inizio dei dolori

è crollato l'ultimo muro
sulle rovine dell'autunno

i bambini lacerati
giocano ancora alla corda
– un vecchio lenzuolo arrotolato –
e il medico rammenda la stoffa ferita
nel rosso dello scarico

forte come la morte
l'amore delle madri
che partorirono l'orma
di questo dolore

è caduta la tegola
che scoppia per aria e corona la terra
unisce i bordi della buca
come un lenzuolo a coprire il corpo
bella rosa della Siria
addormentata in una branda di sangue

alzati amore
dai detriti
alzati
nello sguardo del cielo
che amando genera
alzati

The Fall of the Empire

Every morning
I see him crossing the corner
Between Minerva Square and the Pantheon,
The same grimace
The pace, swift
His grey hair in the wind,
People call him "a loony" or "a nut head,"
His body coated with crusts
A garment he wears with no shame
Perhaps knowing
That teguments change
Waning not the essence

Brother cat listens carefully
To the symphony of his gasps:
Hunger, thirst, sleeplessness

Once someone told me
–that lunatic
walking through the darkest valley
was a hero
in the Holy war–

In awe
I count the centuries
Trapped between clock's needles
I look for the budding dragon
Whose tail will drag the stars,
I find nothing but his eyes

La caduta dell'impero

lo vedo ogni mattina
mentre attraversa l'incrocio
tra Pantheon e Minerva,
la solita smorfia
il passo veloce
e i capelli grigi al vento,
lo chiamano "matto" o "sbroccato",
ha il corpo ricoperto di squame,
un abito che porta con disinvoltura
forse convinto
che i tegumenti mutino
senza intaccare l'essenza

fratello gatto ascolta attento
la sinfonia dell'affanno:
fame, sete e sonno

un giorno qualcuno mi disse
– quel matto
che va per una valle oscura
fu eroe
nella guerra santa –

sbalordita
contai i secoli afferrati alle lancette
cercai
il drago in erba
che con la coda trascina via le stelle,
trovai soltanto i suoi occhi

An explosion of volcanic waters,
The absence of madness
As sharp as the eagle's plunge

Leaving its feathers
In chariot's chest
—he's but a victim of the Empire—
I think
While on his face a smile appears
Restless
      Ludicrous
Just like the judgment
Of prowlers

Translated by the author, Zingonia Zingone

un lampo di acque sulfuree
l'assenza di pazzia
nitida

come l'aquila che scende nell'arca del carro
e ci lascia le piume
– è solo vittima di questo impero –
penso
e sul suo volto si apre un sorriso
agitato
      ridicolo
come il giudizio dei passanti

ABOUT THE EDITOR
MARK LIPMAN

Mark Lipman, founder of the press Vagabond, the Culver City Book Festival, the Elba Poetry Festival; winner of the 2015 Joe Hill Labor Poetry Award; the 2016 International Latino Book Award and the 2023 L'Alloro di Dante (Dante's Laurel – Italy), a writer, poet, multi-media artist, activist, and author of fourteen books, began his career as the writer-in-residence at the world famous Shakespeare and Company in Paris, France (2002-2003). Since then, he has worked closely with such legendary poets as Lawrence Ferlinghetti and Jack Hirschman on many projects and for the last twenty years has been establishing a strong international following as a leading voice of his generation. He's the host and foreign correspondent for the radio program, Poetry from Around the World for Poets Café on KPFK 90.7 FM Los Angeles. As Mark continues to travel the world, he uses poetry to connect communities to the greater social justice issues, while building consciousness through the spoken word.

CIRCA L'EDITRICE
ANNA LOMBARDO

Anna Lombardo: Vive a Venezia. Poetessa, traduttrice e attivista culturale. Laurea in Lingue presso Università Cà Foscari di Venezia; PhD sulla marginalizzazione della scrittura poetica femminile presso il Trinity College di Dublino. Raccolte poetiche bilingue: *Anche i Pesci Ubriachi* (2002); *Nessun Alibi* (2004); *Quel qualcosa che manca* (2009); *Con Candide mani* (2020); *Con cándidas manos* (2023). Ha curato le seguenti antologie: *C'è chi crede nei sogni* (2014); *15x15 la fotografia incontra la poesia* (2020); *La Traduzione al tempo del Covid* (2021). Fin dal 2020, ha ideato e curato quattro antologie dei *Quaderni della Palabra* che raccolgono i lavori presentati dai poeti e dalle poete partecipanti al festival Palabra en el Mundo a Venezia annualmente. Ospite in molti festival internazionali e nazionaliCollabora con il *Global Right* per il quale ha curato sei interviste a poetesse internazionali contemporanee. Lavori critici e di traduzioni di vari autori e autrici, tra i quali: A. Lowell, J. Hirschman, J. Lussu, PP. Pasolini, Chi Trung, e Matt Sedillo. Suoi testi, tradotti in varie lingue sono presenti in riviste ed antologie nazionali ed internazionali. Dal 2009 cura la direzione artistica del FIP (Festival Internazionale di Poesia) *Palabra en el Mundo* per Venezia che annualmente accoglie diverse voci nazionali ed internazionali. È tra i membri fondatori della rete internazionale di poeti e poete POP.

ABOUT THE EDITOR
ANNA LOMBARDO

Anna Lombardo lives in Venice. Poet, translator, and cultural activist. Degree from the Cà Foscari University of Venice with a PhD on the marginalization of female poetry at Trinity College in Dublin. Bilingual poetic collections: *Even the Fish Are Drunk* (2002); *No Alibi* (2004); *That Something Missing* (2009); *Con candide mani* (2020); *Con cándidas manos* (2023). She has edited the following anthologies: *There Are Who Believe in Dreams* (2014); *15x15 photography meets poetry* (2020); *The Translation at the Covid Time* (2021). Since 2020, she has edited the four annual issues of *Quaderni della Palabra*, which collect the works of the poets participating in the *Festival Palabra en el Mundo*. She is a frequent guest at national and international festivals. She collaborates with Global Right, for which she has curated six interviews with contemporary international poets. Various authors' critical and translation works include A. Lowell, J. Hirschman, J. Lussu, PP. Pasolini, Chi Trung, and Matt Sedillo. Her poems have been translated into multiple languages and have been published in national and international journals and anthologies. Since 2009, she has been the artistic director of the FIP (International Poetry Festival) *Palabra en el Mundo* for Venice, which welcomes various national and international voices annually. She is among the founders of the International Poet's Net POP.

EL MARTILLO PRESS

El Martillo Press publishes writers whose pens strike the page with clear intent; words with purpose to pry apart assumed norms and to hammer away at injustice. El Martillo Press proactively publishes writers looking to pound the pavement to promote their work and the work of their fellow pressmates. There is strength in El Martillo.

El Martillo Press titles:

- *From Venice to Venice: Poets of California and Italy*
  edited by Mark Lipman and Anna Lombardo
- *Blackout* by Anna Lombardo
- *A Crown of Flames: Selected Poems & Aphorisms*
  by Flaminia Cruciani
- *detoxification of the body* by gabor g. gyukics
- *Paper Birds: Feather by Feather / Pájaros de papel: pluma por pluma*
  by Sonia Gutiérrez
- *All Brown Boys Get Trumpets* by Matthew Cuban Hernandez
- *Chimeras Dream on Barren Lands* by Alex Alpharaoh
- *the daughterland* by Margaret Elysia Garcia
- *WE STILL BE: Poems and Performances* by Paul S. Flores
- *God of the Air Hose and Other Blue-Collar Poems*
  by Ceasar K. Avelar
- *Touch the Sky* by Donato Martinez

To purchase these books and to keep up with new titles, visit elmartillopress.com.

Milton Keynes UK
Ingram Content Group UK Ltd.
UKHW020948220424
441551UK00019B/1582